TURBINE
POWER

A bold railroading technology
and its fate

On the cover: Union Pacific GTEL No. 12 was captured in Granger, Wyo., in August 1968. *Richard Steinheimer*

Kalmbach Media
21027 Crossroads Circle
Waukesha, Wisconsin 53186
www.KalmbachHobbyStore.com

Published in 2020
24 23 22 21 20   1 2 3 4 5

Manufactured in China

ISBN: 978-1-62700-735-1
EISBN: 978-1-62700-736-8

Editor: Eric White
Book Design: Lisa Bergman

Library of Congress Control Number: 2019943780

TURBINE
POWER

A bold railroading technology
and its fate

Walter Simpson

Kalmbach
Media

Contents

STEL = Steam Turbine Electric Locomotive
GTEL = Gas Turbine Electric Locomotive

Preface

I don't know why I love turbine-powered locomotives and trains. After all, I'm a lifelong environmentalist and energy conservationist. Generally speaking, these machines were not exemplars of energy efficiency and environmental sustainability. But love them I do. Their outrageousness, weirdness, and technical sophistication continually pull me in.

Unfortunately, their story is often ignored or treated as a sideshow because most of them failed to play a significant role moving freight or passengers, and none are operating today. With just a few exceptions, these locomotives and trains never had their heyday, with attempts to develop and operate them occurring primarily in the latter part of the 20th century.

This led me to research and distill the existing literature to create a comprehensive volume, which discusses all American turbine locomotives and trains, hopefully bringing them to life. My goal was to provide enough information and detail to satisfy most readers' curiosity about how these fascinating machines actually worked in all their unusual and sometimes glorious complexity! Additionally, I gathered a large number of photos and other images to make this motive power retrospective engaging and fun.

As an energy professional myself, energy has been my lens. Thus, I've been especially interested in fuel types and energy conservation strategies, as well as overall locomotive energy efficiency. I hope my readers will be also.

While this is a slim volume, much research went into it and I want to share that with my readers. Accordingly, I've provided many endnotes. Additionally, the reading and resources list—a special feature at the end of the book—is as exhaustive as possible and is not found elsewhere.

This book might not be for everyone. But for the right reader with a strong interest in locomotives and railroad history, I trust you'll enjoy it.

Walter Simpson
Amherst, N.Y.
May 19, 2019

Acknowledgments

In researching, writing, and producing this book, I received assistance from many people and organizations. I'm very appreciative of their help. While I take full credit for errors that appear in this book, I want to thank the following people for reading all or part of the manuscript as it evolved and providing helpful comments, suggestions, and corrections—often rescuing me from mistakes on matters where they possess the expertise: Bruce Becker, Mike Bolland, Brian Brundige, Frank Donnelly, Rick Durrant, Don Graab, Arthur Huneke, Mike Iden, Dale Johnson, Dave Keller, Bob Kennedy, Tom Leary, Larry Lohman, Tom Mack, Kenny Mah, Karen Parker, Allen Rider, Peter Roosen, Bryan Schlake, Walter Talbot, Don Wetzel, and Bruce Wolff. I also appreciated my conversations with Johann Stamm regarding his father's involvement with the "Blue Goose" gas turbine locomotive.

Much of my initial fascination with turbine-powered locomotives and trains stemmed from their unique appearance. In telling their stories, it was therefore important to me to include many photographs and other images. I'm very grateful to those who provided images or gave me permission to use them in this book. Their names or organizations are listed throughout the book as photograph or image credits.

Behind these credit lines are many caring people who were especially helpful assisting me find rare or multiple images. Some are already listed above. Additionally, in this regard, I want to offer my thanks to Patricia LaBounty of the Union Pacific Railroad Museum, Patrick Kidd of Amtrak, Jonathan Smith and Chris White of the Jordan Schnitzer Museum of Art at the University of Oregon, Ken Miller and Joe Shaw of the Norfolk & Western Historical Society, Chuck Blardone of the Pennsylvania Railroad Technical and Historical Society, Tom Dixon and Mike Dixon of the Chesapeake & Ohio Historical Society, Bill Vantuono of *Railway Age,* and Diane Laska-Swanke of Kalmbach Media.

I also want to thank Pam Rose for her tireless research assistance and Laura Balcom and my daughter Skye Simpson for their editing assistance, and of course Eric White and Lisa Bergman at Kalmbach for turning my prose into the beautiful book you have in your hands.

Louis M. Newton's extraordinary first-hand account of testing the Norfolk & Western's "Jawn Henry" steam turbine electric locomotive (*Rails Remembers, Volume 4—The Tale of a Turbine*) played a major role awakening my interest in turbine-powered locomotives. I offer him special thanks for inspiration. Dale A. Johnson's much more recent and excellent *Trail of the Turbo: The Amtrak Turboliner Story* also showed me what a book about turbine locomotives and trains could aspire to. I am indebted and grateful to so many other individuals whose previous research and writings on this subject matter made my own project possible.

This book, like my previous one on diesel-electric locomotives, is dedicated to my wife, Nan, whose love and support made it possible. My debt to her is many, many train rides long!

Baldwin Locomotive Works produced this brochure for the June 23-27, 1947 track exhibit in Atlantic City, N.J. Railroads such as the Chesapeake & Ohio were hoping to keep coal as a relevant railroad fuel, leading in this case to the development of the M-1. *Courtesy of Chesapeake & Ohio Historical Society (cohs.org).*

1
Turbine locomotives and trains

Turbine-powered locomotives and trains (hereafter referred to as turbine locomotives and turbine trains) incorporate steam or gas turbines in their propulsion system. While their existence paralleled the steam, diesel-electric, and electric locomotive eras, they played a far less significant role in American railroading. Today in the United States, turbine locomotives and trains are out of use, so in a sense they are historical artifacts. Nonetheless, their narratives are compelling and interesting.

As we shall see, some American turbine locomotives were developed in the 1940s and '50s with the hope of maintaining coal as a viable locomotive fuel, while delaying dieselization[1]. But eventually the fate of these and other turbine locomotives was decided on a purely practical (economic) basis.

The railroads selected fuel and technology combinations that produced the least expensive and most reliable motive power. On that basis, most turbine locomotives and trains didn't make the grade, with the prime exceptions being the Union Pacific gas turbine locomotives and the Amtrak Turboliners.

Diesel-electric locomotives using diesel engines as their prime movers[2] to generate electricity onboard were generally more cost effective and became predominant in the railroad industry. However, none could match the top speed of a few of the gas turbine locomotives discussed later in this book. Straight electric locomotives found a niche in passenger service along the Pennsylvania Railroad's New York to Washington D.C. main line, now known as the Northeast Corridor, as well as in many urban and commuter rail systems.

The Hoover Dam of Motive Power

"If we may paraphrase Mr. (Robert) Frost, something there is that doesn't like a turbine locomotive. On blue-print paper a turbine has much to recommend itself: it eschews pistons and rods and crankshafts and like reciprocating bric-a-brac; it isn't persnickety about its diet; and it produces horsepower with the gusto of Hoover Dam."

—*David P. Morgan, Editor*
Trains magazine 1953-1987

David P. Morgan wrote at least six articles for *Trains* magazine on turbines.

1 Turbine trains and locomotives classified						
Fuel	Coal	Coal	Diesel Fuel	Diesel Fuel	No. 6 Fuel Oil	Natural Gas
Drive Type	Direct Drive	Electric Transmission	Mechanical/ Torque Converter	Electric Transmission	Electric Transmission	Electric Transmission
Steam Turbine	PRR S2	C&O M-1 and N&W TE-1 STEL			UP STEL 1+2	
Gas Turbine		UP 80+80B GTEL	MTA GT-1, Amtrak UAC, RGT, RLT Turboliners	MTA GT-2 and GT/E trains, Bombardier JetTrain GTEL	UP Big Blow GTEL, Westinghouse-Baldwin "Blue Goose" GTEL	Compressed Integrated Natural Gas Locomotive (proposed)

Turbine trains discussed in this book are primarily Amtrak's gas turbine-powered trainsets which operated between 1968 to 2003. Here, the term trainset refers to a train whose power units and passenger cars are semi-permanently connected and there is a power unit or locomotive on both ends of the train. Trainsets didn't need to have power units configured this way, but the turbine-powered trains discussed in this book do.

Types of turbine locomotives and trains

The technological variety of turbine locomotives and turbine train power cars can make them difficult to understand. They can be categorized according to these classes:
- Turbine—steam or gas
- Energy source—coal, diesel fuel, or Bunker C no. 6 fuel oil, etc.
- Transmission—direct drive, torque converter, or electric transmission

The chart, **1**, places the turbine locomotives and turbine train power cars discussed in this book within their proper class or category, where STEL means steam turbine electric locomotive and GTEL means gas turbine electric locomotive. Both are explained below.

The New York Central Railroad's jet-powered Budd Rail Diesel Car and a proposed atomic steam turbine locomotive, both also discussed in this book, are not included in this chart.

The New York Central wanted to test the physics of high-speed trains on jointed rail and used a jet-powered Budd Rail Diesel Car to go more than 180 mph. *Tom Miller*

Turbine locomotive and train operators

The American railroads that operated turbine locomotives and trains included:
- Pennsylvania RR (PRR)
- Chesapeake and Ohio Ry. (C&O)
- Norfolk & Western Ry. (N&W)
- Union Pacific RR (UP)
- New York Central RR (NYC)
- Long Island RR (LIRR)
- Penn Central Transportation Company (Penn Central)
- Amtrak

In its search for greater power and cost-savings, Union Pacific experimented with and/or used three different turbine locomotive types. Amtrak operated three different types of TurboTrains and Turboliners.

Turbine locomotive and train builders

The manufacturers that built turbine locomotives or trains (or significant components) included:
- Baldwin Locomotive Works
- Westinghouse
- Baldwin-Lima-Hamilton
- Babcock & Wilcox
- General Electric
- American Locomotive Company
- United Aircraft Corporation
- ANF Industrie
- Rohr Industries
- Bombardier
- Alstom

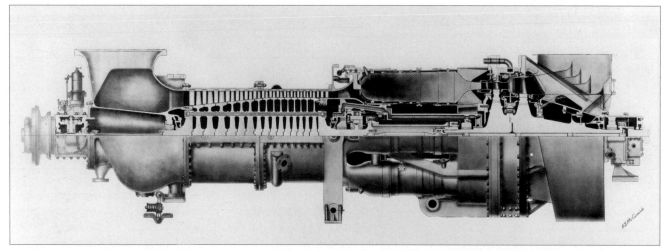

This partial cutaway view shows the General Electric 4,500 horsepower gas turbine engine for one of the first Union Pacific gas-turbine electric locomotives. The air intake is at the left end, exhaust is at the right. A gearbox attached to the central shaft reduced the RPM level to match the generator. *General Electric*

Turbine fuel choices

These fuels were used to "fire" steam and gas turbine locomotives and turbine train power cars:

- Coal
- Bunker C No. 6 fuel oil
- Diesel fuel

The coal used in steam turbine locomotives was burned in firetube and watertube boilers. When used in a gas turbine, this solid fuel had to be pulverized into a fine powder, an approach that did not produce positive results. Some railroads owned coal supplies and thus had an incentive to developed coal-fired locomotives of more advanced designs to maintain coal-burning.

The most famous fuel oil-burning gas turbine locomotives were the Union Pacific's "Big Blow" GTELs. These burned No. 6 fuel oil, also known as Bunker C fuel oil. Bunker C is a heavy residual oil and, as such, is a residue of the oil-refining process. Residual fuel oil is what is left over after lighter oil molecules (groupings of which are called fractions) have evaporated and condensed in refinery fractionating columns, producing gasoline, naphtha, kerosene, diesel fuel, lubricating oil, and other fractions. Bunker C is so heavy and viscous that it needs to be heated to flow. Most other petroleum-burning turbine locomotives burned diesel fuel, a distillate petroleum product because it is produced by distillation in the fractionating column.

Heavy fuel oil was used in many oil-burning steam locomotives, such as Southern Pacific Cab Forwards. Southern Pacific also converted approximately 50 Electro-Motive Division F7 A and B-unit diesel locomotives to operate on heavy fuel oil between 1956 and 1957.[3] The locomotives had dual fuel tanks—one containing 350 gallons of diesel fuel (for starting the diesel engine, bringing its cooling water up to 160°F, and stopping the engine) and the other containing 1,150 gallons of residual fuel oil. Additional hot water piping was installed to overcome fuel oil's high viscosity[4]. Union Pacific also used Bunker C fuel oil in some specially modified diesel-electric locomotives in the 1950s and 1960s[5].

The gas turbines used in Amtrak's TurboTrains and Turboliners were originally helicopter engines. For railroad use they were adapted to use diesel fuel instead of kerosene-based aviation fuel.

Transmission types

Turbine locomotives and turbine train power cars used these mechanisms to transmit the power produced by their turbines to the rail:

- Direct drive
- Torque converter
- Electric transmission

In a turbine locomotive or power car with a "direct drive" transmission, the output shaft of the turbine was connected to the drive wheels directly through a series of gears. These gears stepped down, or reduced, the high rotational speed of the turbine to lower speeds, which were matched to the top speed of the locomotive.

A turbine locomotive or power car with a torque converter (also known as a torque coupler) transferred the turbine's mechanical energy to the locomotive's wheels using a fluid coupling. This coupling allowed for an incremental transfer of torque or rotational force. A common torque converter is incorporated in an automobile's automatic transmission. Locomotives with torque converters also used step-down gearing.

An electric transmission is used in diesel-electric locomotives, and was also used in some turbine locomotives and trains. One or more electric generators, traction motors, gears, bearings, wheels, and associated circuitry comprise this type of transmission.

In a diesel locomotive, the generator is rotated by the locomotive's diesel engine, while in a turbine locomotive a steam or gas turbine served as the locomotive's prime mover and rotated the generator.

Step-down gearing was needed in turbine-powered locomotives to connect the shaft of the turbine to the generator because of the high speed of the turbine. As previously mentioned, a steam turbine locomotive with an

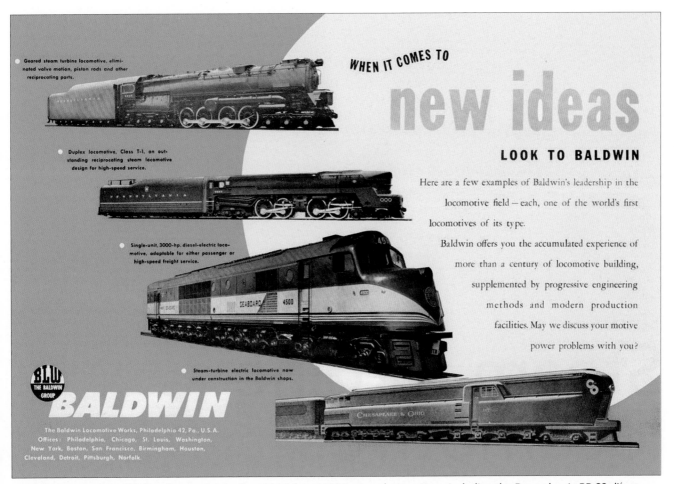

A Baldwin Locomotive Works ad promotes its "modern" (late 1940s) steam locomotives, including the Pennsylvania RR S2 direct-drive steam turbine and C&O M-1 STEL, in an era of dieselization. *Courtesy of Chesapeake & Ohio Historical Society (cohs.org).*

electric transmission was called a steam turbine electric locomotive or STEL. A gas turbine locomotive or power car with an electric transmission was called a gas turbine electric locomotive or GTEL.

Energy transformations
A number of energy transformations occur within turbine locomotives and power cars. They begin when a screw or pump draws chemical energy in the form of coal or oil from the locomotive's bunker or fuel tank and sends it to either the boiler in a steam turbine locomotive or combustion chambers in a gas turbine locomotive.

The heat energy in the steam or combustion gases is then transformed into mechanical energy when it forces a steam or gas turbine to rotate. The turbine shaft may be mechanically connected to the locomotive's drive wheels (through direct drive gears or a torque converter) or to the rotor of a generator (in locomotives with an electric transmission). In the latter, electrical energy is produced to power the locomotive's electric traction motors, which then produce the mechanical energy that propels the locomotive and its train.

2

Steam turbine locomotives

The use of steam turbines to provide motive power for railroad locomotives was not invented or first tried in the United States. One noteworthy earlier prototype was the Swedish Ljungström steam turbine locomotive described in a 1923 *Popular Mechanics* magazine article.[6]

This 126-ton, 72-foot-long steam turbine locomotive was credited with cutting coal consumption in half while producing 1,800 horsepower, 24,000 pounds of tractive effort (i.e. the force delivered to the locomotive's wheels for propulsion), and a top speed of 60 mph.

Power was supplied to the drive wheels through a direct drive mechanism with double-reduction gearing. The locomotive also featured a large water condenser (to recover and reuse boiler water) and a turbine-powered induction fan for its combustion air heater. Overall, a clever design.

The American steam turbine locomotives discussed in this chapter were developed and operated between 1939 and 1957.

Advantages and disadvantages

These were the anticipated (hoped for) primary advantages of turbine locomotives:

• Better Fuel Economy. Proponents of American coal-burning steam turbine locomotives of the 1940s and '50s hoped there would be a significant improvement in efficiency compared to the 7% to 8% overall best efficiency of conventional reciprocating-engine steam locomotives.

• Lower Overall Cost. Steam turbine proponents hoped to achieve overall operating, maintenance, and purchase/depreciation costs equal to or less than diesel-electric locomotives.

• Continued Use of Coal. For the coal industry and railroads heavily invested in coal, perpetuating the use of coal as the principal locomotive fuel was a primary objective.

However, projected energy efficiency gains did not materialize. Steam turbine locomotives were also maintenance headaches. As a result, they did not achieve anticipated benefits compared to diesel-electric locomotives.

How steam turbines work

Steam turbines are essentially enclosed paddlewheels that spin at high speed when jets of highly pressurized steam strike the cupped ends of their turbine blades, forcing rotation and producing shaft horsepower. They convert heat energy into mechanical energy.

When steam turbine locomotives were being proposed, there was substantial familiarity with steam turbine technology because it had already been used for years in stationary electrical generating plants. There was, however, an open question whether it could be effectively applied to locomotives, which operate in a mobile and generally harsh railroad environment.

Popular Mechanics Magazine

REGISTERED IN U. S. PATENT OFFICE

WRITTEN SO YOU CAN UNDERSTAND IT

Vol. 39	FEBRUARY, 1923	No. 2

Turbine-Driven Locomotive Cuts Coal Consumption in Half

By GEORGE F. PAUL

A TURBINE-DRIVEN locomotive embodying such radical departures from accepted designs as to form a decided innovation in the field of locomotive engineering, has been developed in Sweden. When it is remembered that an ordinary locomotive turns only about 6 per cent of the heat of its coal into useful work, whereas in modern power plants from 10 to 20 per cent of the heat of the coal is utilized, it is evident that the locomotive offers great scope for improvement.

This new locomotive is 72 feet long over all, and weighs, in running order, 126 tons. The motive power is a steam turbine capable of developing 1,800 horsepower. This turbine drives the three pairs of coupled wheels by means of double-reduction gearing. The turbine is carried on the front end of what one is tempted to call the tender. In reality it is the engine part of the complete locomotive. It embodies the whole of the driving mechanism and auxiliary apparatus, as well as the condensing plant. The front part of the locomotive carries the boiler, with superheater, the turbine-driven induced draft for the air heater, and the coal bunker. The latter is in the form of a saddle tank, and has a capacity of seven tons of coal. The tractive effort of the locomotive is 12 tons, and the maximum speed 60 miles an hour.

It should also be noted that the de-

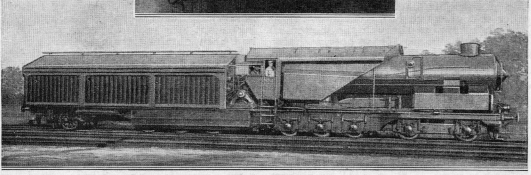

Above: View of Turbine-Driven Locomotive, Showing Main Turbine, Reduction Gears, and Control Apparatus. Below: Side View of Locomotive, the Front Part of Which Carries the Boiler, Superheater, Induced-Draft Fan, Air Heater, and Coal Bunker, While the Rear Carries the Power Equipment and Condensing Apparatus

165

The February 1923 *Popular Mechanics* magazine reported on an early steam turbine locomotive. This unique locomotive was equipped with an 1,800 horsepower steam turbine and a steam condensing tender that recovered water and heat for reuse. Fuel efficiency was 12%, compared to 6% for conventional steam locomotives. *Courtesy of Popular Mechanics magazine*

This Siemens SST-800 steam turbine is a modern unit designed for stationary electrical generation. Energy in high-pressure steam is converted to rotational power by many stages of precisely curved turbine blades. The "bucket" size and wheel diameter increase as the steam pressure and density reduce. Steam flow in this turbine starts near the upper worker's left hand and passes through the steam turbine's high-pressure section on the right-hand side of the photo. Steam flow is then reversed and redirected to the medium- and low-pressure sections on the left side of the photo. *Siemens*

Steam turbine locomotive energy efficiency

Steam turbines have played an important role in stationary electric power plants and marine applications where their efficiency can be maximized. But applying this technology to locomotives was challenging.

The steam turbines used in the locomotives discussed here achieved less than 20% efficiency. In other words, under the best conditions (what can be called design conditions), they wasted over 80% of the energy in the steam they produced.

Generally speaking, steam turbine locomotives were inefficient because they exhausted huge volumes of steam that still contained much of its energy. However, at least one such locomotive, Union Pacific's Bunker C fuel oil-fired STEL, was designed to recover some of that energy by condensing waste exhaust steam and using the energy in it to preheat boiler feedwater.

It takes a lot of energy to produce steam from water—970 BTUs per pound of water. Condensing the steam releases that energy, some of which can then be captured and reused.

However, while steam turbines operate with maximum efficiency at full speed and load, their efficiency decreases when speed and load decrease. Thus, steam turbine efficiency tended to be poor under normal locomotive operating conditions, including starting, stopping, varying speeds, and changing loads.

The further loss in efficiency during normal operation could be dramatic such as in the case of the Pennsylvania RR's class S2 6-8-6 direct-drive steam turbine locomotive. The steam consumption of this locomotive at 5 mph was four times greater than that of a highly wasteful conventional steam locomotive with similar boiler capacity at that speed.[7] However, at full speed and load, the S2 was more efficient.

Of course, the efficiency of the

steam turbine itself was only part of the turbine locomotive's efficiency story. The energy efficiency of an entire locomotive was a function of the efficiency of the turbine multiplied by the efficiency of the boiler (which would include the firebox) and the efficiency of the rest of the locomotive's drivetrain.

For a direct drive steam turbine locomotive, the rest of the locomotive's drivetrain would be the gears, bearings, and wheels. If the design or peak efficiencies of these components were representative values—such as 75% for the boiler, 17% for the steam turbine, and 95% for the gears and bearings—then the design fuel-to-rail efficiency of this locomotive would be 12.1%, calculated as follows:

$$0.75 \times 0.17 \times 0.95 = 0.121 \text{ or } 12.1\%$$

For a steam turbine locomotive with an electric transmission, the rest of the locomotive's drivetrain would be its

A Baldwin Locomotive Works builder photo shows the inner workings of the M-1 locomotive's 6,000 horsepower steam turbine and double armature generator. Each armature was capable of producing 2,000 kw of electrical power. *Chesapeake & Ohio Historical Society (cohs.org).*

How steam power plants achieve higher levels of efficiency

Stationary steam power plants now achieve average annual energy efficiencies of 33% to 60% or more.[8] They accomplish this in a variety of ways, the most significant being the capture and reuse of low-pressure steam exiting the power plant's primary, or high pressure, steam turbines. Lower pressure steam still contains significant energy. This energy can be extracted by a series of lower-pressure turbines. Further using waste heat to provide process and district heating additionally increases overall steam plant efficiency.

One reason that steam turbine locomotives did not utilize multiple, cascading turbines to improve efficiency was that the locomotives did not have sufficient "real estate." There just wasn't enough room within an already crowded, very large locomotive to do so. Other factors included locomotive cost, complexity, and maintenance requirements.

electric generator, traction motors, gears, bearings, wheels, and associated circuitry and controls. The electric transmission efficiency of early diesel-electric locomotives with DC traction motors was typically assumed to be 82%.

Using that efficiency, a STEL operating in its most energy efficient design condition range with the same 75% efficient boiler and a 17% efficient steam turbine would have a design fuel-to-rail energy efficiency of 10.5%, calculated as follows:

$$0.75 \times 0.17 \times 0.82 = 0.105 \text{ or } 10.5\%$$

While STEL design efficiency is less than that of the direct drive steam turbine locomotive, STELs were overall more efficient in practice because they were better at maintaining efficiency at slower speeds and partial loads.

Design condition efficiencies of steam turbine locomotives were better than those of conventional steam locomotives, but not by much. In real life operation (under typical railroad conditions), the average efficiency of steam turbine locomotives could be much less than conventional steam locomotives.

Noteworthy examples of steam turbine locomotives

The four steam turbine locomotives described on the following pages are presented in chronological order based on the date of delivery of the first locomotive of their classes. Unless otherwise noted, horsepower data are for the steam turbines only, not horsepower as delivered to the generators or the rail.

The first locomotive discussed represents General Electric and Union Pacific's initial attempt to use a turbine prime mover with very inexpensive Bunker C heavy residual fuel oil (1939-1943); a much more successful GE/UP gas turbine effort was to follow.

The Pennsylvania RR then tried a Westinghouse-Baldwin-built, coal-fired steam turbine locomotive, the S2, that produced a lot of horsepower and could run very fast but did not perform well enough in other respects for a second one to be built (1944-1949).

Following these efforts were two more Baldwin-built steam turbines. These were STELs—the Chesapeake and Ohio's M-1 passenger locomotive (1947) and the Norfolk & Western's TE-1 freight locomotive (1954-1957). While fascinating machines, neither locomotive performed well enough to save the day for coal-burning locomotives or stop the diesel locomotives from becoming the railroad industry's motive power of choice.

In 1939 Union Pacific received two 2,500 horsepower Bunker C fuel oil-fired STELs from General Electric. Billed as steam-electric power plants on wheels, these locomotives were geared for 125 mph and expected to routinely pull heavy 12-car passenger trains at 110 mph on flat terrain with twice the efficiency of conventional steam locomotives. Working together as a 5,000 horsepower pair, it was also anticipated they would be able to pull these trains up steep 2.2% grades without the assistance of additional locomotives, known as helpers.

These STELs incorporated many energy conservation features.[10] In addition to burning inexpensive Bunker C fuel oil, they used water-tube Babcock & Wilcox boilers with efficiency features that included:
• Very high-pressure steam—1,500 psi (920°F) compared to 300 psi steam in the most efficient conventional steam locomotives
• Advanced controls that automatically increased and decreased the boiler firing rate to match load
• Superheaters that passed steam through additional boiler tubes to increase its temperature and pressure
• An economizer heat exchanger that captured and used exhaust stack waste heat to preheat boiler feedwater
• An air preheater heat exchanger that captured and used exhaust stack waste heat to preheat boiler combustion air

The high-pressure steam produced by the boiler fed a single two-stage steam turbine that rotated two generators whose main job was to provide electricity to the locomotive's

Bunker C fuel oil-fired steam turbine electric locomotives[9]
• 1939-1943
• 2,500 horsepower
• Two locomotives designed and built by General Electric and Babcock & Wilcox
• Operated by Union Pacific and Great Northern

Union Pacific No. 2 was photographed in Denver on May 27, 1939. Air vents for steam condensing coils are evident at the rear of the locomotive. *Louis A. Marre collection*

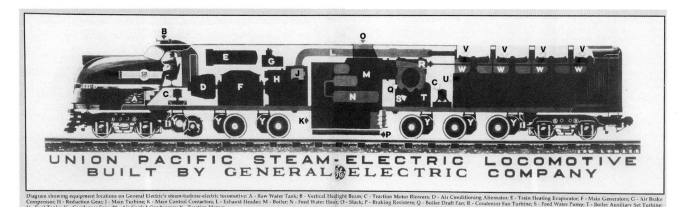

UNION PACIFIC STEAM-ELECTRIC LOCOMOTIVE
BUILT BY GENERAL ELECTRIC COMPANY

Diagram showing equipment locations on General Electric's steam-turbine-electric locomotive: A - Raw Water Tank; B - Vertical Headlight Beam; C - Traction Motor Blowers; D - Air Conditioning Alternator; E - Train Heating Evaporator; F - Main Generators; G - Air Brake Compressor; H - Reduction Gear; J - Main Turbine; K - Main Control Contactors; L - Exhaust Header; M - Boiler; N - Feed Water Heat; O - Slack; P - Braking Resisters; Q - Boiler Draft Fan; R - Condenser Fan Turbine; S - Feed Water Pump; T - Boiler Auxiliary Set Turbine; U - Fuel Tanks; V - Condenser Fans; W - Air Cooled Condensers; Y - Traction Motors.

Trains magazine collection

electric traction motors. Exhaust steam from the main steam turbine was piped to low-pressure turbines connected to other equipment (called auxiliaries) and an evaporator that provided steam for passenger car heating.[11]

While this locomotive was designed to both burn inexpensive fuel and be energy efficient, getting all this sophisticated equipment to work properly proved difficult.

Bunker C cost a few pennies per gallon compared to 10 to 12 cents per gallon for diesel fuel at the time. Moreover, each gallon of Bunker C contained more energy than a gallon of diesel fuel, i.e., 150,000 BTUs vs. 138,000 BTUs, respectively. That added to its potential cost-effectiveness.

However, Bunker C's price and energy density advantages came with disadvantages that were costly. This fuel is so resistant to fluid flow that it has been described as one step short of asphalt. Because of its thick, tar-like viscosity, it must be heated to flow.

The energy required to heat the fuel was an energy loss—a parasitic load—because it did not directly power the locomotive. More than that, failure to maintain the heating of Bunker C in cold weather could produce catastrophic results, plugging up every piece of equipment through which it otherwise flowed.

To conserve energy and water, these steam turbine locomotives used a closed loop system with large condensers, **1.** By condensing the steam in this configuration, the steam turbines could

operate with greater efficiency[12] and boiler feedwater could be recycled.

The condensers consisted of finned heat exchangers mounted in the back of the locomotive. Steam was condensed in heat exchanger pipes using a steam turbine-powered fan to blow ambient air across them. Vanes on the sides of the locomotive would open and close to modulate air flow for the condensation process. The closed water loop was reported to contain 3,000 pounds (359 gallons) of water that was continuously reused.[13]

At full power output, the boilers could evaporate the water in the closed loop in just three and a half minutes. Thus, for this locomotive to work properly at full power (and not run out of water), its condensers had to be able

Union Pacific No. 1 sits in Northwestern Station in Chicago on April 30, 1939. *Harold Mummer/Trains magazine collection*

The Union Pacific oil-fired STELs were designed to pull passenger trains at over 100 mph across the Midwest, and up 2.2% grades in the West without helper locomotives. This image was a popular one for advertising. *Union Pacific/Trains magazine collection*

Union Pacific's steam turbine-powered locomotive is featured in this 1939 Socony-Vacuum Oil Co. print advertisement that appeared in the May 1939 issue of *Engineering and Mining Journal*. The ad notes that each turbine will consume 1,500 psi steam and develop 2,500 horsepower at 12,000 rpm. Socony-Vacuum is credited with developing just the right oil to be "light enough to lubricate the turbine ... yet heavy enough to protect precision reduction gears." *Courtesy of ExxonMobil Corporation*

to condense and recover water from turbine exhaust steam at this same rapid rate. This was no small feat.

While there were some water losses, these were modest by steam locomotive standards and were replenished by a 4,000-gallon "raw water" tank located in the nose of the locomotive. This STEL was designed to travel 500 to 700 miles between water stops, a big plus given the arid nature of parts of Union Pacific's cross-country routes. Large conventional steam locomotives carried over 20,000 gallons of water in their tenders yet required water at much shorter intervals.

The locomotive's condenser represented both water and energy conservation technology. Instead of allowing all of the thermal energy in the steam to escape to the atmosphere, it retained the warm condensed water and then reheated it in the economizer with energy recovered from the condensation process itself.

The water was then reinjected into the boiler for another cycle of boiling, turbine-twisting, and condensation. By introducing already hot water into the boiler, less energy was needed to convert it to steam.

Interestingly enough, boiler feedwater in this locomotive was also heated by dynamic braking. When this type of braking was used, the locomotive's electric traction motors functioned as generators. The electricity they produced was dissipated as waste heat by resistors placed into contact with the feedwater.[14]

Despite all of their innovative

Let us stand up and cheer!

"American inventive genius never has been, is not now, and probably never will be satisfied with a single achievement. Always it must learn something new from what it has already done and then go on to something better. Therein lies one great reason for its matchless record for nearly 300 years. This indomitable determination to make something new and better has touched every phase of our national life and enriched it beyond measure. And that is why, in the field of transportation, we now come face-to-face with a splendid new transcontinental steam-electric locomotive that almost stuns our admiration into silence and finally makes us want to stand up and cheer for the men who made it."

—*Stanley A. Dennis*, Science and Mechanics *magazine, April 1939*

features and design cleverness, UP returned these steam turbine locomotives to GE the same year it received them. There were too many problems making them work properly and economically. These experimental locomotives just could not compete with UP's other steam motive power at the time: the 4-8-8-4 Big Boy and 4-6-6-4 Challenger steam locomotives and the new General Motors Electro-Motive Division (EMD) E and F type diesel-electric locomotives.[15]

The STELs were then further tested on New York Central's Water Level Route in New York, and then were used by the Great Northern RR for freight service from 1941-1943 during World War II, after which the locomotives were again returned to GE and permanently retired.

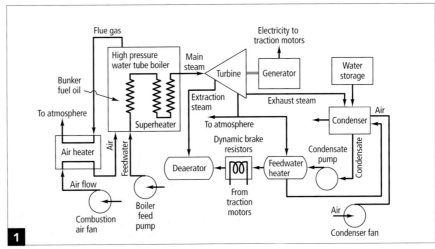

1

Power generation flow chart for Union Pacific Bunker C fuel oil-fired steam turbine electric locomotive. *Walter Simpson*

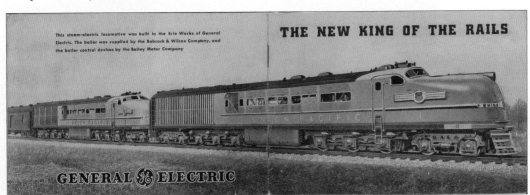

THE NEW KING OF THE RAILS

This steam-electric locomotive was built in the Erie Works of General Electric. The boiler was supplied by the Babcock & Wilcox Company, and the boiler control devices by the Bailey Meter Company

GENERAL ⓖ ELECTRIC

This GE brochure circa 1940 heralds its new steam turbine electric locomotive as the "King of the Rails." The locomotive was a technological tour de force, and arguably ahead of its time, but it was not reliable enough for railroad service. *General Electric*

The locomotive consists of two of these units. Each is rated 2500 hp and can operate independently. The door in the "nose" opens into a passage to the operator's cab. One of the two headlights throws a beam straight upward as a warning signal when running in deep canyons through mountainous districts.

AMERICA'S FIRST   STEAM-ELECTRIC

Another great advance in the forward march of American railroading! Steam and electricity work together to drive a railroad locomotive—steam, traditionally the source of locomotive power, and electricity, the smoothest and quietest means of transmitting that power. Built in the General Electric shops at Erie, Pa., this locomotive represents the co-operative efforts of General Electric and Union Pacific research engineers

in doing what had never been done before anywhere in the world—installing a high-pressure, condensing turbine-electric power plant in a railroad locomotive. They had a big job. They succeeded, as is proved by the locomotive's exceptional performance on test runs. It will do twice the work of the conventional steam locomotive for each pound of fuel. It will go three times as far without stopping for fuel or water.

Engineers like to run this locomotive. The one shown here is at the electric controls, which include accelerating, reversing, and braking. The power plant is completely automatic. The phone at his left is for talking with other members of the train crew.

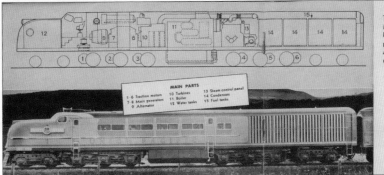

MAIN PARTS

1-6 Traction motors 10 Turbines   13 Steam control panel
7-8 Main generators   11 Boiler   14 Condensers
9 Alternator   12 Water tanks   15 Fuel tanks

The locomotive is in two units, one of which is shown at the left. In each unit a steam turbine drives an electric generator which supplies current to the six electric motors on the axles. The information below applies to each unit.

Top speed—125 mph
Power—2500 hp
Weight—265 tons
Length—90 ft, 10 in.
Height—15 ft
Width—10 ft
Fuel used—low-grade oil ("Bunker C")
Fuel capacity—3000 gal
Water capacity—4000 gal
Steam conditions—1500 lb per sq in. at 920F
Traction generators and motors—direct-current
Auxiliary power—220 volts, alternating current
Mileage between water or fuel stops—500 to 700 miles

EXAMPLE 2: PENNSYLVANIA RR S2 COAL-FIRED STEAM TURBINE LOCOMOTIVE

Direct-geared steam turbine locomotive[16]

- 1944-1949
- 6,900 horsepower
- Coal-fired
- A single locomotive designed and built by Westinghouse Electric and Manufacturing Company and the Baldwin Locomotive Works
- Operated solely by the Pennsylvania RR

The PRR's one-of-a-kind, 6-8-6 steam turbine locomotive had a large fire-tube Belpaire boiler[17] with a 120-square-foot grate area, which produced 310 psi steam. It was connected to two Westinghouse steam turbines: a 6,900+ horsepower turbine for forward motion and a 1,500 horsepower turbine for reverse.

It was direct drive with the turbine output shafts physically connected to the locomotive's middle two drive axles by double-reduction gears. These gears were substantial, designed to handle the locomotive's abundance of power.[18] Side rods connecting the locomotive's eight drive wheels ensured that all of them (and four axles) were effectively driven.

While the S2 looked pretty much like a conventional steam locomotive it didn't make chuffing sounds or emit smoke from its stack in spurts because it didn't have front-mounted pistons that abruptly vented exhaust steam twice per drive wheel revolution.

Instead, the S2's power delivery and exhaust were of a continuous smooth nature. This was a big plus for the tracks because smooth delivery of power eliminated most rail-pounding, the damaging uneven forces applied to the rails by the piston strokes of reciprocating steam locomotives.

However, the continuous nature of the S2's exhaust did pose a problem for firebox drafting. With no spurts of steam exiting the smoke stack there were no spurts of combustion air being

The *Manhattan Limited* leaves Chicago Union Station with a 14-car train in June 1947. The 1,500 horsepower reversing steam turbine is evident on the left side of the Pennsylvania RR class S2 6-8-6 along with the steam line feeding it from the front of the boiler. *PRRT&HS/The Keystone*

The S2 is in Denholm, Pa., on its initial run to Harrisburg. *Pennsylvania Railroad Technical & Historical Society/The Keystone*

pulled through the firebox to fan the flames of coal combustion. That put a damper on steam production despite this locomotive's giant appetite for steam.

There was also a concern that the lower velocity draft would lead to an accumulation of ash in the boiler's combustion chamber and firetubes. To solve this problem, multiple small steam exhaust nozzles were installed in the locomotive's smoke box. Like when putting your finger over just part of the end of a garden hose, these nozzles restricted turbine exhaust steam flow to increase its escape velocity.[19]

However, while improving draft, fuel burn, and power, this solution imposed back pressure on the turbine which tended to reduce energy efficiency. (Note that steam nozzles were not a new idea. They were used on conventional reciprocating steam locomotives to increase draft as well.)

This steam turbine locomotive gained the nickname "Battleship" because its steam turbine technology was adapted from marine applications. Like a battleship, it was also very powerful. It was capable of pulling heavy passenger trains at 110 mph and able to operate at full power more

efficiently than conventional steam locomotives.[20]

But the S2 was doomed by its high steam consumption and much lower efficiency when starting and at low and medium speeds.[21] When it started, steam consumption by its primary turbine was reported to be so high that it would cause boiler pressure to drop precipitously while simultaneously spinning its drive wheels.[22]

The S2 exceeded the efficiency of conventional steam locomotives at speeds above 70 mph[23] and exceeded the power of a four-unit diesel locomotive, which would produce

Pennsylvania RR No. 6200 sits in Chicago on July 15, 1945. It would run until 1949 before being scrapped. Visible on the right side is the 6,900 horsepower forward movement steam turbine. Note the massive steam line. *PRRT&HS/The Keystone*

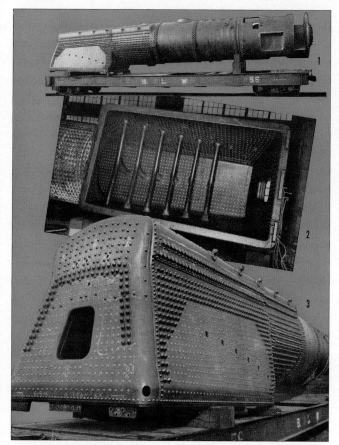

A page from a Baldwin S2 steam turbine brochure depicts the locomotive boiler on a flatcar and a bottom view of the room-sized firebox revealing six thermic siphons that allowed boiler water flow through the boiler. This improved steam production and efficiency. *Baldwin Locomotive Works/author's collection*

SOMETHING NEW IN LOCOMOTIVES

POWERED LIKE A BATTLESHIP

Jets of steam, racing at 2000 miles per hour through a turbine no larger than an office desk, provide 6500 horsepower for this Pennsylvania Railroad giant, the first direct drive steam turbine locomotive to be produced in the United States.

Built by Baldwin with turbines and gears made by Westinghouse, it represents an adventure in steam locomotive construction, opening the way to desired higher speeds and greater operating efficiency.

It is natural that Baldwin, a leader in locomotive development for more than a century, should have pioneered in this radically new type of steam locomotive.

But this is not the whole story. Baldwin hydraulic machinery, testing equipment, ship propellers, diesel engines and other products are serving industry in a hundred useful ways.

BALDWIN

The Baldwin Locomotive Works, Philadelphia, Pennsylvania: Locomotive & Ordnance Division; Baldwin Southwark Division; Cramp Brass & Iron Foundries Division; Standard Steel Works Division; The Whitcomb Locomotive Co.; The Pelton Water Wheel Co.; The Midvale Co.

BALDWIN SERVES THE NATION | WHICH THE RAILROADS HELPED TO BUILD

Baldwin Locomotive Works played on wartime sentiment in this magazine advertisement announcing its new steam turbine locomotive. The slogan "powered like a battleship" was used because the steam turbine was the same type used in battleships. *Baldwin Locomotive Works/author's collection*

6,000 horsepower at speeds above 40 mph. The S2's turbine produced 7,240 shaft horsepower on the Pennsylvania RR's Altoona, Pa., locomotive dynamometer.[24] In 1947, it was reported that no other non-electric locomotive could develop that much horsepower above 70 mph.[25]

While the S2 concept never would have produced an energy efficient locomotive, it could have been more efficient if PRR/Baldwin had selected a water-tube boiler capable of producing much higher steam pressure.

However, reasons for not using a water-tube boiler on this locomotive probably included: (1) to keep new design elements to a minimum and (2) to provide reserve steam capacity. Maintaining reserve steam capacity was critically important because of the S2's excessive consumption of steam when starting, accelerating, and at lower speeds.

The S2 prototype locomotive ran just five years and 106,000 miles (an average of less than 60 miles per day) before being retired in 1949. It was an interesting experiment, but was considered a failure because of unresolved maintenance issues and overall poor energy efficiency. Moreover, like all of these coal-fired steam turbine locomotives, its timing was bad. It wasn't possible to compete with the new diesel-electric locomotives.

Pennsylvania RR's triplex locomotive design concept[26]

The next two steam turbine locomotives, the Chesapeake & Ohio M-1 and Norfolk & Western TE-1, looked like giant shoe boxes. The precedent for their boxy shape and layout was the PRR's "Triplex" locomotive proposal. This locomotive, which never reached construction, would have been another 100-mph, direct-geared, coal-burning steam turbine locomotive. Theoretically, it would have developed an incredible 9,000 horsepower from two turbines, yielding 8,100 drawbar horsepower. Drawbar horsepower is the horsepower measured at the drawbar or coupler of the locomotive connecting it to the train it's pulling. Above 30 mph, the Triplex would also have produced more drawbar tractive effort than the most powerful conventional steam locomotives, Chesapeake & Ohio's Allegheny 2-6-6-6 and PRR's Q2 2-4-6-4 steam locomotives.

This locomotive was called a triplex because it would have been a three-part locomotive: the coal bin, engineer's cab and boiler, and the water tender with the first two parts supported by the locomotive's mainframe. The triplex's layout placed the engineer and fireman somewhat closer to the front of the locomotive than they would have been in an equally powerful conventional steam locomotive. This provided marginally better visibility while still allowing access to the boiler.

The mainframe's wheel configuration was given as 4-8-4-8. The 8-wheel trucks were to be powered. Their four axles would have been driven by a steam turbine through flexible drives with gearing to achieve the locomotive's 100 mph top speed. The PRR proposal addressed the problem of traction loss that would have occurred as the coal bunker emptied and thereby reduced weight on the lead power truck. This was done by progressively pumping water from the tender into auxiliary tanks located in the front part of the locomotive.

Interestingly enough, the PRR considered the Triplex locomotive to be a steam turbine counterpart to the railroad's highly successful GG1 electric locomotive.[27] While PRR advertising stated that this "radically new" steam turbine locomotive was "actively being progressed,"[28] it died on the vine, probably a victim of dieselization. The Triplex did, however, set the stage for the C&O's M-1 and Norfolk & Western's TE-1 – though these locomotives would be STELs, not direct-drive locomotives.

The giant steam turbine "Triplex" will cover nearly 137½ feet of track, with a wheel base of 122½ feet. As here pictured, the front is to the right; note that the cab is located *ahead* of the boiler.

Pennsylvania Railroad

The backhead of No. 6200 is equipped with a profusion of gauges and valves to monitor and control the locomotive. The backhead, shown while under construction at Baldwin Locomotive Works on October 10, 1944, is the firebox end of the boiler in the S2 locomotive's cab. *PRRT&HS/The Keystone*

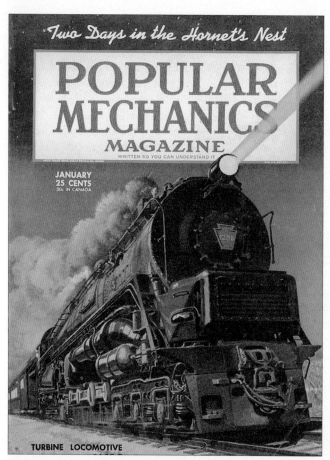

The S2 steam turbine locomotive graced the cover of *Popular Mechanics* in the January 1945 issue. The machine was unable to live up to the expectations for it. *Popular Mechanics*

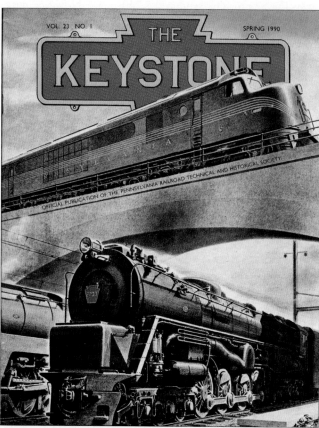

The Pennsylvania RR's S2 steam turbine locomotive is featured on the cover of the spring 1990 edition of *The Keystone*, the magazine of the Pennsylvania RR Technical & Historical Society. This artwork was produced by Baldwin Locomotive Works in 1946 for the cover of its *Baldwin* magazine. On the bridge above the S2 is a Baldwin "Centipede" diesel-electric locomotive. *PRRTHS/The Keystone*

S2 steam turbine: coal's new hope

"The ultimate status of the steam locomotive is hard to predict. Some feel confident that its day is done. Others feel that any (railroad) which buys anything but steam is a victim of super-salesmanship. My own feeling is largely this:

The steam locomotive today is a remarkably effective means of moving rail traffic. It has a background extending over a century. Admittedly, it has its faults, but it also has many proved virtues. High on the list of virtues are its low first cost and ability to burn either coal or oil. I think it would be unfortunate for the American railroad industry if development in steam power did not continue to keep pace with development in other types of locomotive (motive power)."

—*Charles Kerr Jr., consulting transportation engineer, Westinghouse Electric and Manufacturing Corporation, 1947*

EXAMPLE 3:
CHESAPEAKE & OHIO
COAL-FIRED M-1 STEL

M-1 No. 500 pulls a heavyweight test train near Low Moor, Va., in December 1947. *Chesapeake & Ohio Historical Society (cohs.org)*

Steam turbine electric locomotives[29]
- 1947-1948
- 6,000 horsepower
- Coal-fired
- Three locomotives designed and built by Baldwin Locomotive Works and Westinghouse Corporation
- Operated solely by the Chesapeake & Ohio RR

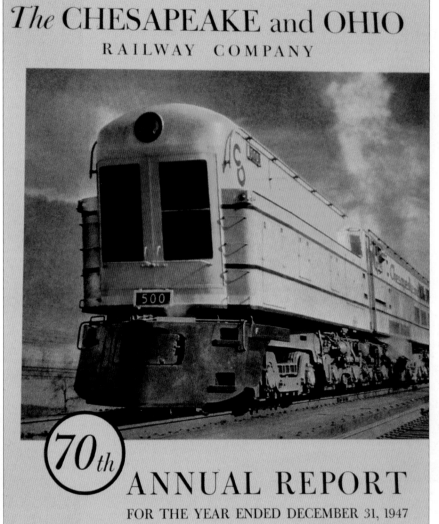

The big beautiful orange prow of the M-1 graces the cover of C&O's 70th annual report in 1947. *Chesapeake & Ohio Historical Society (cohs.org).*

The Baldwin Locomotive Works C&O M-1 brochure from the June 23-27, 1947, track exhibit in Atlantic City, N.J., shows the location of the "principal parts" of the locomotive. *Chesapeake & Ohio Historical Society (cohs.org).*

In the 1940s, the Chesapeake & Ohio spoke altruistically about the need to perpetuate coal-burning locomotives because oil supplies could dry up in 30 years. But the company's commitment to coal was profoundly a matter of self-interest. The C&O, self-described as the "Coal Bin of America," was then the largest originator of bituminous coal in the world.[30] Thus, it wasn't surprising that C&O partnered with Baldwin and Westinghouse to develop a new type of coal-burning steam locomotive when presented with the reality of successful dieselization.

The first of these locomotives, No. 500, was delivered in 1947, with No. 501 and No. 502 arriving in 1948. These three monstrous 145-foot-long,[31] 857,000-pound, coal-burning STELs would each be equipped with a 6,000 horsepower steam turbine connected to two "double armature" 2,000 kilowatt electric generators. The drawbar horsepower of these locomotives would prove to be 4,488 horsepower at 41 mph.[32]

The three M-1s were intended to pull the C&O's most prestigious passenger train—the *Chessie*, running between Washington, D.C., and Cincinnati, Ohio—at speeds approaching 100 mph. However, their timing was all wrong not just because of the onslaught of diesel-electric locomotives but also because passenger rail travel was steadily declining after World War II.

In PRR Triplex fashion, the M-1's cab was in the middle of the locomotive. The coal hopper was in the front, and the locomotive's boiler, steam turbine, electrical generators, and other equipment were located in the rear.

Like the PRR S2, the C&O M-1 was equipped with a 310 psi firetube boiler. This avoided new technology but similarly settled for reduced energy efficiency. The locomotive's tender carried a 25,000-gallon water supply which the M-1 could consume in less than two and a half hours.[33]

The designers attempted to make this big box locomotive look attractive and aerodynamic by smoothing its corners, leaning its prow forward as though it were cutting through the air. Its livery

On the move, M-1 No. 502 is pulling a new streamlined train at Clifton Forge, Va., in 1948. *Chesapeake & Ohio Historical Society (cohs.org).*

was a lively yellow/orange and white.

Chesapeake & Ohio's steam turbine locomotives were delivered with an unusual asymmetrical running gear configuration. While the locomotive's lead "power unit" comprised a four-wheel leading truck and an eight-wheel power truck, its rear power unit comprised a four-wheel leading truck, an eight-wheel power truck, and a four-wheel trailing truck—creating a first-of-its-kind 4-8-0-4-8-4 wheel arrangement. Its eight traction motors were claimed to deliver 98,000 pounds of starting tractive effort and 48,000 pounds of continuous tractive effort.

The men in the C&O shops referred to these new locomotives as "sacred cows," while the company sought to get as much public relations credit from them as possible. The first locomotive was sent on a system-wide publicity tour that allowed 40,000 people to meet the locomotive and walk through its cab.

But in the end, the effort put into promoting these locomotives didn't produce meaningful results. The complicated and new M-1s were unreliable and difficult to maintain. Other problems included excessive coal and water consumption, slippage, and poor drafting. Consequently, and apparently unceremoniously, the three

An artist's preliminary drawing of the M-1 locomotive shows how an aerodynamic shape was formed to enclose the bulky machinery. *Chesapeake & Ohio Historical Society (cohs.org).*

RAILROAD

35 CENTS   MAGAZINE   AUGUST

The August 1948 cover of *Railroad Magazine* featured this striking M-1 painting by Frederick Blakeslee. These locomotives burned dirty coal but cleaned up nicely. *White River Productions*

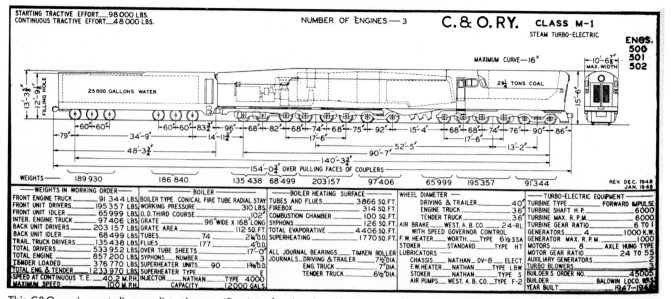

This C&O equipment diagram lists the specifications for the class M-1 locomotive. *Chesapeake & Ohio Historical Society (cohs.org).*

Crowds line up to view the cab of C&O No. 500 on a publicity tour, designed to create renewed interest in passenger rail travel. This M-1 is on display in Waynesboro, Va., in 1948. *Chesapeake & Ohio Historical Society (cohs.org).*

The "Plumber's Nightmare." The M-1 is shown with its cowl removed and blowing off some steam. These STELs were not of simple design nor easy to maintain. *Chesapeake & Ohio Historical Society (cohs.org)*.

locomotives were quickly retired and scrapped in 1950 without ever fully realizing their performance and energy efficiency potential.

While viewed as experimental, C&O scholar Gene Huddleston described riding behind these locomotives when they were operating impressively, and stated that they ranged throughout C&O's territory for two years.[34] In contrast, author Geoffrey George said the M-1s "wheezed erratically" in mainline performance, a reference to the locomotive's drafting problems.[35]

With this intriguing locomotive and others discussed in this book, it's tempting to say: "Too bad one was not saved for posterity!" But railroads were and continue to be big businesses, typically not as sentimental about old or failed locomotives as the railfan community. The tangible dollar value of scrapping was greater than the abstract value of historical preservation.

Chesapeake & Ohio M-1 No. 501 waits at the engine servicing terminal at Cincinnati Union Terminal in June 1949. One of three of the class, their designed purpose of hauling luxurious passenger trains never panned out as the market for rail passengers was shrinking as the 1950s dawned. *David P. Oroszi collection*

While railfans regret that all three M-1s were scrapped, railroads take a dollar and cents approach and are not sentimental about outmoded equipment. *Chesapeake & Ohio Historical Society (cohs.org)*.

The strange story of the *Chessie*—a train that never ran

The three M-1 steam turbine electric locomotives were constructed to pull new, futuristic C&O passenger trains at high speeds through the Allegheny Mountains on a route running between Washington, D.C., and Cincinnati, Ohio. The 599-mile route was to be completed in 12 hours, averaging a very challenging 60 mph, including stops. The train was called the *Chessie*. Three complete 14-car trainsets (plus extra cars) were delivered to the C&O in 1948 by the Budd Company, but the *Chessie* never ran once in revenue service.

The *Chessie* and its unique turbine locomotives were the brainchild of C&O board Chairman Robert R. Young. He took the reins in 1942 and held that position for 12 years before leaving to head the New York Central. During his time at the C&O, Young sought to remake the railroad in a variety of ways. Achieving national leadership in passenger rail travel was a particular passion. The modern and luxurious *Chessie*—designed to surpass all other passenger trains—was central to that aspiration.

In a well-written, detailed account of the *Chessie* story for *Trains* magazine, Geoffrey H. George described plans for these trains.[36] Each would have:

- A nurse and a passenger representative in addition to other railroad staff
- Coach cars seating 36 passengers (compared to standard 42 or 52)
- Reserved seating
- 10-position reclining seats with built-in speakers for radio and music listening
- Venetian blinds on windows
- Individual lockers in each coach car
- A library for borrowing books
- Writing desks next to women's lounges
- Toilets with ultraviolet germ-killing lights
- A lounge car with plantings, a fountain, and a goldfish tank
- Eight-seat lounges in each luxury coach
- High-quality original oil paintings depicting scenes along the *Chessie* route
- A family coach car for those with children, equipped with a cartoon theater, playpens, cradles, and diaper-changing areas
- Twin dining cars with seating for 52 that converted to movie theaters after meals
- Two lunch counters with snack bars
- Two dome cars (showing off "some of the best landscape in the East")
- An all-daylight time schedule
- Absolutely first-class service

This astonishing list suggests that the *Chessie* would be an unstoppable winner. Unfortunately, Young's dream was financially unsupportable. The chairman of the board had misread the post-WWII passenger rail market. It wasn't expanding; it was contracting. Moreover, the Washington-Cincinnati route was definitely not the best proving ground for a re-invigorated passenger rail service. Sadly, the *Chessie* proved an embarrassing chapter for the C&O as well as a source of substantial financial loss. Without these special trains to pull, the troublesome M-1 locomotives were superfluous.

C&O board Chairman Robert R. Young explains the fittings of the Chessie's "cabin" rooms to a radio host in 1947. The train was intended to be a leader in passenger rail travel, but came as interest in train travel was declining. *Trains magazine collection*

While the C&O called itself the "Coal Bin of America," in this print ad it depicted itself as one with nature. The ad actually sought to convey that C&O passenger trains were the "finest fleet of air-conditioned trains in the world." In the era of coal-fired steam locomotives, air-conditioning was synonymous with in-car cleanliness because it allowed passenger car windows to remain closed. *Chesapeake & Ohio Historical Society (cohs.org)*

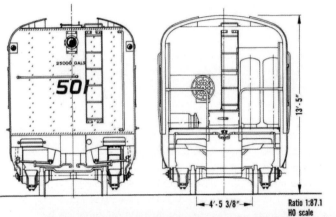

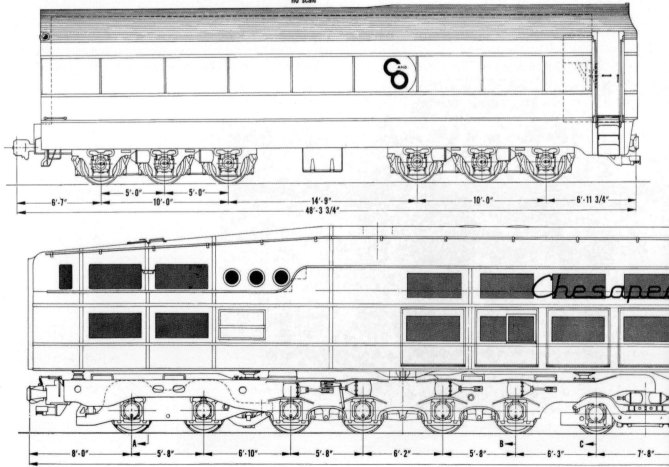

WORLD'S *LARGEST* PASSENGER LOCOMOTIVE

ON EXHIBITION CHICAGO RAILROAD FAIR

THE Chesapeake and Ohio Railway's "500" is the first coal-burning steam turbine-electric locomotive ever built and the largest passenger locomotive in the world.

It is revolutionary in design, combining three well-tested principles—the conventional steam boiler, the steam turbine and electric drive.

Considered separately, none of these principles is new. It is the combination of them that makes this locomotive radically different from other coal-burners.

Briefly, the "500" operates in this manner: Its coal-fired boiler produces steam that is conducted to the turbine. The 6,000 horsepower turbine drives twin generators which produce 4,000 kilowatts of electrical energy. These generators power eight motors which deliver a total of 4,960 horsepower to the 16 driving wheels.

The new giant of the rails differs radically in size, weight and arrangement from the standard reciprocal drive steam locomotive.

The "500" is 140 feet, 3-3/4 inches long, including locomotive and water tender. The engine alone weighs 411-1/2 tons, and is geared for a top speed of 100 miles per hour.

The arrangement of the "500" is like nothing else on the rails. The usual coal-burning locomotive has the boiler in front of the cab and the coal bunker in the tender at the rear. The "500" has a 29-1/4-ton coal bunker ahead of the cab, and a 25,000-gallon water tender coupled back of the locomotive. An automatic stoker feeds coal from the bunker, passing it under the cab into the fire box immediately behind the cab.

This locomotive has many operational advantages over its predecessors. Its electric drive assures operating flexibility, smooth starting and full power at all operating speeds.

The C & O "500", together with its companion locomotives, numbers "501" and "502", comprise Chesapeake and Ohio's powerful new fleet of steam turbine-electric locomotives.

Chesapeake & Ohio described the M-1 as "the first coal-burning steam turbine locomotive ever built and the largest passenger locomotive in the world" in its 1948 Chicago Railroad Fair brochure. *Chesapeake & Ohio Historical Society (cohs.org).*

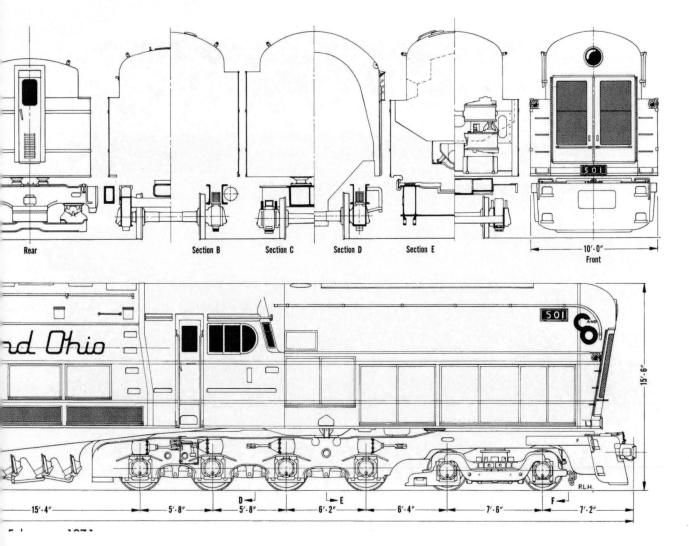

Rear Section B Section C Section D Section E 10'-0" Front

15'-4" 5'-8" 5'-8" 6'-2" 6'-4" 7'-6" 7'-2"

15'-6"

EXAMPLE 4: NORFOLK & WESTERN COAL-FIRED TE-1 STEL

Steam turbine electric locomotive[37]
- 1954-1957
- 4,500 traction horsepower
- Coal-fired
- One unit designed and built by Baldwin-Lima-Hamilton Locomotive Corporation, Westinghouse, and Babcock & Wilcox Company
- Operated solely by the Norfolk & Western RR

As the last major Class 1 railroad to give up on coal-burning and steam power, Norfolk & Western was really committed to coal and steam. The railroad also had ample experience with all-electric locomotives in its most mountainous territory. No wonder then that N&W was interested in developing a coal-fired steam turbine electric locomotive.

To save the day for coal, N&W knew it had to demonstrate that such a locomotive could be much more energy efficient than a conventional steam locomotive. Baldwin, Westinghouse, and Babcock & Wilcox believed such a locomotive could be built and worked closely with N&W to develop and test the TE-1, where "T" and "E"

apparently stood for "turbine" and "electric."

In 1954, Baldwin-Lima-Hamilton delivered a single 818,000 pound, 111-foot-long prototype locomotive with a 6-6-6-6 wheel configuration to N&W. Even longer than the C&O M-1, the TE-1 stretched to 161 feet with its water tender. It was given the number 2300 and nicknamed *Jawn Henry* after the legendary African-American track worker John Henry of "steel driving" fame.[38]

In layout, the *Jawn Henry* was similar to the C&O's M-1. However, the 4,500 horsepower TE-1 was a freight locomotive designed to produce much higher levels of starting and continuous tractive effort than the M-1.

Norfolk & Western's TE-1 is shown in a publicity photo. The coal bin and the dynamic braking grids are in front of the cab. Behind it are the high-pressure boiler, steam turbine, electrical generators. *Norfolk & Western Historical Society*

TE-1 No. 2300 makes an early appearance with Class J 4-8-4 No. 605 in Roanoke, May 17, 1954. The TE-1 was designed to haul heavy coal trains from the mines to tidewater for the Norfolk & Western Ry. *Norfolk & Western Historical Society*

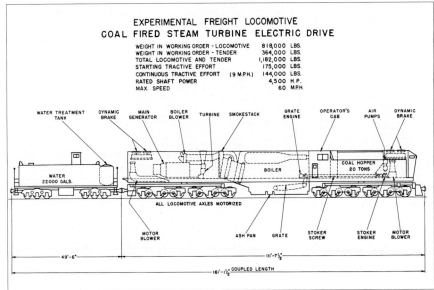

EXPERIMENTAL FREIGHT LOCOMOTIVE
COAL FIRED STEAM TURBINE ELECTRIC DRIVE

WEIGHT IN WORKING ORDER - LOCOMOTIVE	818,000 LBS.
WEIGHT IN WORKING ORDER - TENDER	364,000 LBS.
TOTAL LOCOMOTIVE AND TENDER	1,182,000 LBS.
STARTING TRACTIVE EFFORT	175,000 LBS.
CONTINUOUS TRACTIVE EFFORT (9 M.P.H.)	144,000 LBS.
RATED SHAFT POWER	4,500 H.P.
MAX. SPEED	60 M.P.H.

Norfolk & Western Historical Society

TE-1 main turbine and generators. The steam turbine, 1, is on the right; the gearbox, 21, is in the middle; and the auxiliary and main generators, 17, 18 and 19, are on the left. The turbine-like device on top, 14, is actually a combustion air blower. *Baldwin-Lima-Hamilton Operator's Manual, author's collection*

The TE-1 produced 175,000 pounds of starting tractive effort vs. 98,000 pounds for the M-1, and 144,000 pounds of continuous tractive effort vs. 48,000 pounds for the M-1. The TE-1 had 12 traction motors, one per axle. Maximum speed was 60 mph. The locomotive's coal bunker capacity was 20 tons.

Jawn Henry's superlative tractive effort was sufficient for it to pull a coal train with 134 loaded cars over a mountain division. It could also exert enough force to split trains apart by breaking their couplers.[39] On one occasion, when starting a train at 1 mph, the TE-1 achieved a measured tractive effort of 199,000 pounds,[40] an amount of pulling power characteristic of AC diesel-electric locomotives 40 years later.

This tractive effort was significantly greater than N&W's conventional steam locomotive tractive champion, the 2-8-8-2 Y6b/c, which had demonstrated 152,000 to 166,000 pounds of tractive effort.[41]

As a STEL, the TE-1 was equipped with dynamic brakes. These, as previously explained, converted the locomotive's electric traction motors so they would function as generators. In this mode, the traction motors applied a resistive force to the axles and wheels, slowing the train while generating electricity. This electricity was dissipated to the atmosphere as waste heat through blower-cooled dynamic braking resistor grids, located at the top of the locomotive at the ends.

The TE-1 was designed to be as energy efficient as possible within the physical constraints of the locomotive. Among its efficiency measures was a water-tube boiler that provided 600 psi (900° F) steam, a feedwater preheater, and a combustion air heater.

While the use of high-pressure steam had thermodynamic advantages, it increased the chances of leaks and required higher-cost materials and construction. Also, steam leaks in 600 psi systems cannot be seen at their point of origin because steam under that pressure does not condense immediately. The "invisibility" of steam leaks posed a danger to maintenance staff and operators.

The TE-1 is pulling a dynamometer car and coal train on an early shakedown run in Elliston, Va., on June 2, 1954. *Norfolk & Western Historical Society*

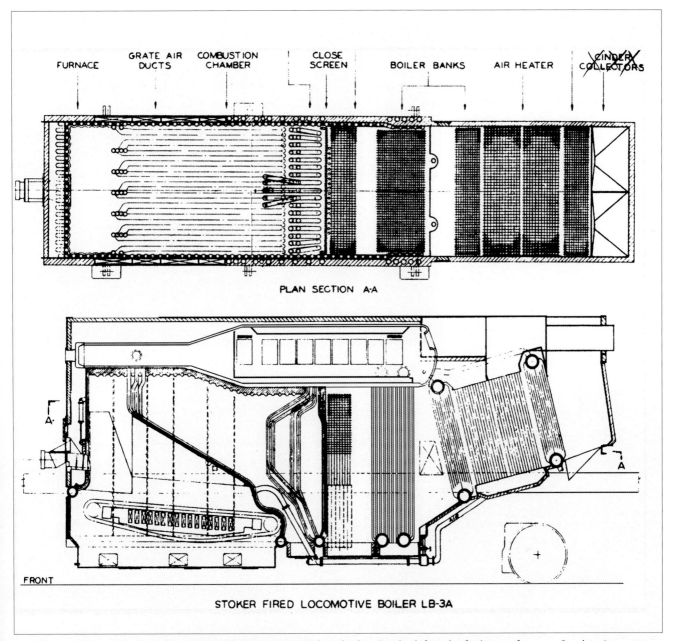

FURNACE   GRATE AIR DUCTS   COMBUSTION CHAMBER   CLOSE SCREEN   BOILER BANKS   AIR HEATER   CINDER COLLECTORS

PLAN SECTION A·A

A·

FRONT

A

STOKER FIRED LOCOMOTIVE BOILER LB-3A

Top view and longitudinal section views of the Babcock & Wilcox boiler. On the left is the firebox or furnace. Combustion products released from burning coal are conducted up and over an arch to extend burning time in what is called the combustion chamber portion of the firebox. The large gas heater for preheating combustion air is shown on the right. Boiler exhaust exits on the far right. *Norfolk & Western Historical Society*

Jawn Henry's specifications called for a Type 43A Worthington feedwater preheater. Worthington feedwater heaters were "open type," where cold feedwater from the tender was pumped to the locomotive smoke box where it was sprayed through the locomotive's exhaust steam before being injected into the boiler.

This contact with the steam not only warmed the feedwater, it also condensed some of the steam, which could be then recycled into feedwater (reducing

locomotive water consumption). Feedwater heaters generally reduced coal consumption by about 10%.

The combustion air heater, alternately called an air heater or gas heater, was a huge heat exchanger in the exhaust portion of the boiler. It captured waste heat from the boiler's exhaust and used it to preheat combustion air.

This heat exchanger was a four-pass counterflow design.[42] Combustion air was propelled through it by a steam

turbine-driven fan. By one account, this gas heater preheated combustion air to 350°F.[43] However, Baldwin Locomotive Works specifications stipulated that the combustion air would be heated to 500°F.

Approximately half that heated air would then be cooled (using ambient air) to 300°F for introduction under the firebox grates. The other half of the 500°F air was introduced at the firebox arch to boost combustion of volatile coal gases, thereby improving efficiency.[44]

Hot combustion products released from burning coal below were forced through this maze of tempering air tubes inside the top portion of the TE-1's firebox before encountering the water tubes of the boiler. *Norfolk & Western Historical Society*

Jawn Henry pulls a test train at Riverside, Va. The men on the top of the locomotive are standing in the coal bunker shoveling coal onto a scale during an efficiency test in 1954. *Norfolk & Western Historical Society*

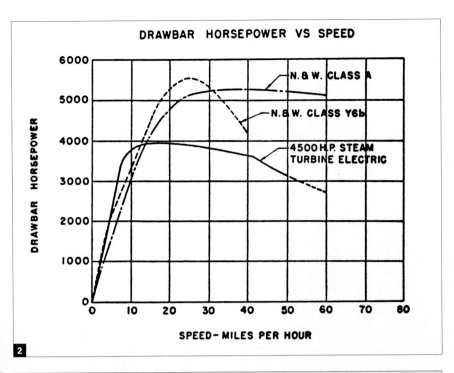

DRAWBAR HORSEPOWER VS SPEED

N. & W. CLASS A

N. & W. CLASS Y6b

4500 H.P. STEAM
TURBINE ELECTRIC

These horsepower curves for the TE-1 and N&W's other powerful freight locomotives, the 2-8-8-2 Class Y6b and the 2-6-6-4 Class A, show that while the TE-1 could produce greater tractive effort than the other two locomotives, the Y6b and A had greater horsepower above 14 mph, enabling them to haul heavy trains faster over a given route. *Norfolk & Western Historical Society*

When mineral scale builds up in a boiler's water tubes, heat transfer is reduced, adversely impacting steam production and efficiency. To avoid this condition, the TE-1's feedwater was treated by a Zeolite water softening system in the 22,000-gallon tender.

Norfolk & Western required Baldwin, as lead contractor, to produce a locomotive that would achieve 11% efficiency "between the coals and the rail."[45] While this level of efficiency may seem poor, it would have been nearly 50% better than the 7% to 8% best efficiency of conventional steam locomotives.

In order to demonstrate that the 11% efficiency had been achieved, the contract stipulated that Baldwin-Lima-Hamilton had to demonstrate 12.1% efficiency at the generator output.[46] This goal was reached during tests conducted May 12 to 14, 1954, when a full-load test yielded 12.17% efficiency at the generator output.[47] From an operating perspective, the part-load test results were as important as the full-load test results. These were less impressive, 11.66% at two-thirds load and 9.76% at one-third load, but still much better than a conventional steam locomotive.[48]

During testing, Baldwin demonstrated that these component efficiencies were achieved:

Boiler—75.5% efficiency49
Steam Turbine—16.9% efficiency50
Electrical Generator—92.2% efficiency51

Multiplying these component efficiencies yields an overall 11.8% efficiency, which is close to the 12.17% coal-to-generator efficiency indicated above and required by contract.

0.755 x 0.169 x 0.922 = 0.118 or 11.8%

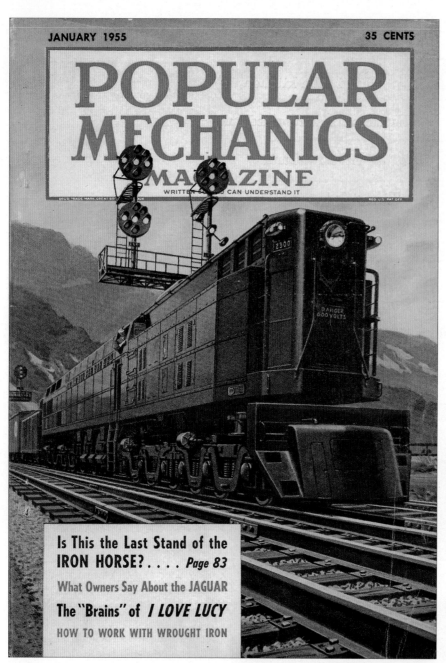

Jawn Henry as possibly "the last stand of the iron horse," *Popular Mechanics*, January 1955. *Popular Mechanics*

Steam turbine energy losses could have been reduced by recovering some of the heat in the turbine's steam exhaust being vented to the atmosphere. One analysis concluded that the overall (fuel-to-rail) efficiency of the TE-1 could have been boosted from 11% to 16% if it was designed to recover heat from the turbine's steam exhaust using an air-cooled condenser similar in concept to those used in Union Pacific's previously discussed unsuccessful STELs.[52] However, this would have required an even longer

locomotive with a specially designed tender. As it was, the TE-1 was already too long to be turned on N&W's turntables.

Theoretically, energy from the turbine's steam exhaust also could have been recovered by mimicking a stationary steam power plant and sending the steam exhaust to a second (low-pressure) turbine that would generate additional electricity for use by the locomotive. But, as previously explained, this strategy would have required additional space within the

locomotive. Plus, there would have been more complexity, impacting reliability and maintenance.

Most of the power produced by locomotive prime movers directly serves tractive purposes, though some is siphoned off to run auxiliary equipment. In the case of *Jawn Henry*, smaller turbines tied to auxiliary functions consumed 170 horsepower worth of steam.[53] Boiler combustion air drafting problems were addressed with a forced-draft boiler blower.

While improved energy efficiency

The N&W used yellow flags on pushers to denote the rear of the movement. This photo was made at Shaffers Crossing in Roanoke, Va., April 1, 1954, and the TE-1's last movement was backing down Blue Ridge and thus the flag was on the front coupler. The locomotive would operate in helper service out of Roanoke at the end of its career before being scrapped in 1958.

Norfolk & Western Historical Society/Louis Newton

and high levels of starting and low-speed tractive effort were of special interest to N&W, the railroad made a profit by being able to move tonnage at speed. That required horsepower.

The challenging N&W Radford, Va., route was chosen for test runs. On these runs, the TE-1 burned less fuel and could handle heavier tonnage than N&W's Y6b steam locomotive. But when both locomotives were tested with 10,000-ton trains, the TE-1 could not match the Y6b's speed in completing the run.[54]

In fact, above 14 mph, both the Y6b and N&W's other powerful articulated locomotive, the 2-6-6-4 A Class, could produce more horsepower and thus tractive effort-at-speed than the TE-1, **2**. For these tests, peak drawbar horsepower of the TE-1, the Y6b, and the A Class were 4,000 horsepower at 18 mph, 5,500 horsepower at 25 mph, and 5,300 horsepower at 36 mph, respectively.[55]

The January 1955 cover of *Popular Mechanics* featured a color illustration of the *Jawn Henry* locomotive and asked, "Is this the last stand of the iron horse?" Despite the article's optimism, it was, in fact, the last stand for the steam locomotive and it didn't last long.

Jawn Henry ran in pusher service on the Blue Ridge grade east of Roanoke. There, turning the locomotive around was unnecessary and it was a short

Baldwin's attempt to market next-generation STELs[60]

Early optimism about the *Jawn Henry* led N&W's superintendent of motive power in Roanoke, Va., to meet with representatives of Baldwin-Lima-Hamilton to discuss mutual interest in building more of these locomotives, though with added horsepower and other modifications.[61] Cost reduction associated with orders of up to 60 new STELs was considered.

This discussion led to an April 14, 1955, conference between Baldwin and Norfolk & Western and Union Pacific railroads, the latter having also indicated potential interest in acquiring a number of high-horsepower coal-burning STELs.[62] A brief report, dated May 25, 1955, was issued by Baldwin following that conference. The report stated that at the conference Union Pacific requested that Baldwin investigate the feasibility of a one-unit locomotive with 7,000 traction horsepower (i.e. horsepower delivered to the generators) and 6,000 horsepower at the rails. A separate tender would be added to that single unit. Norfolk & Western stated that a two-unit locomotive (plus tender) was acceptable and the locomotive should have 6,000 to 6,500 traction horsepower. Both companies wanted the design to incorporate a condensing turbine as well as other features.

A condensing steam turbine provides increased energy efficiency by achieving a greater differential between steam inlet and outlet pressures. This is accomplished by having a water-cooled condenser reduce the temperature (and therefore pressure) of the steam exiting the turbine. The condensing heat exchanger creates this partial vacuum using recirculated cooling water that absorbs heat from the steam. This heat is then rejected into the atmosphere by another set of coils assisted by fans. With this equipment, the condensing water loop can continuously provide cool water to the condenser in a separate closed loop cycle that does not consume (i.e. dump) the cooling water.[63]

In a stationary power plant, heat rejection to the atmosphere occurs in giant cooling towers. In the steam turbine electric locomotive envisioned by Baldwin the "cooling tower" would be incorporated into an evaporative cooling tender.

Baldwin concluded that the high horsepower STELs UP and N&W expressed interest in would have to be two-unit locomotives plus tender. These units would be (from front to back):

- Auxiliary Unit—Operator's cab and 30-ton coal bin
- Main Power Unit—Electrical controls, air compressor, boiler, turbine power plant; 12 traction motors
- Tender—Evaporative cooler; 30,000-gallon water storage

The overall length of this behemoth, including tender, would be 271 feet. Concerning the locomotive's great size and power, Baldwin provided this interesting statistic: The horsepower-to-length ratio would be 7,000 horsepower ÷ 271 feet = 25.8. To put this statistic in context, we can compare it to the horsepower-to-length ratio of UP's 4-8-8-4 Big Boy steam locomotive, which probably would have been replaced by this STEL. The Big Boy with tender was 132 feet long. Its power is generally given as 6,300 horsepower, for a horsepower-to-length ratio of 6,300 hp ÷ 132 feet = 45.45 – almost double that of the STEL. What the STEL would provide, however, was twice the energy efficiency and thus half the coal consumption.

These speculative discussions between Baldwin and the railroads didn't go anywhere. With the reality of dieselization setting in, not one additional high-horsepower STEL was built.

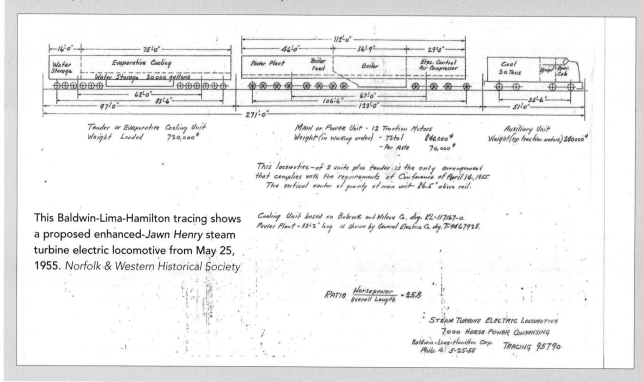

This Baldwin-Lima-Hamilton tracing shows a proposed enhanced-*Jawn Henry* steam turbine electric locomotive from May 25, 1955. *Norfolk & Western Historical Society*

"By the middle of July 1954, the sights and sounds of the 2300 were becoming familiar to people along the way between Roanoke and Bluefield. Instead of the staccato exhausts of conventional steam power, it emitted a combination of sounds: the hissing of steam from the turbine exhaust, the roar of the forced-draft boiler blower, and the whine of the traction motor blowers. In dynamic braking, there was an additional whine from the cooling fans. The whistle was somewhat of a disappointment. Set in a well atop the boiler, its sound was rather coarse. At any rate, the new locomotive was at least being tolerated if not welcomed with great enthusiasm by those concerned with its operation. But, as we heard from time to time from various sources, it still had to 'prove itself.' "

—*Louis M. Newton,*
Rails Remembered, Volume 4 –
A Tale of a Turbine *(page 804)*

Having completed its task as a helper, the 2300 drifts down the mountain to assist the next train. *Norfolk & Western Historical Society.*

Louis M. Newton

trip to the shops when repairs were needed. The locomotive was retired in 1957 after operating 60,000 miles[56] and scrapped in 1958. The decision not to order more TE-1s from Baldwin-Lima-Hamilton was reached just before N&W began its transition from coal-fired steam locomotives to diesel-electric locomotives.

To its credit, the TE-1 was much more reliable than the C&O's M-1 and able to perform actual railroad work. But it was also beset by maintenance problems pertaining to the turbine, generator, feedwater pump, and controls. It was often sidelined.

While N&W's operating department may have wanted to order more locomotives like *Jawn Henry* (see "Baldwin's attempt to market next-generation STELs"), management did not. C.E. Pond, Norfolk & Western's general manager for motive power and equipment (1953-1967) gave these reasons[57] for not buying more locomotives of this type:

• High locomotive purchase price due to custom-built nature, complexity, and weight
• Control failures resulting in added maintenance and loss of availability
• Long length of the locomotive and tender, which meant it could not be turned on N&W's standard turntables
• Insufficient thermal efficiency
• Not cost-competitive with diesel-electric locomotives

Louis M. Newton, a 37-year veteran of railroad service with N&W and then Norfolk Southern, is the TE-1's most authoritative commentator. He was involved in all aspects of the TE-1's testing and development, described in his *Rails Remembers, Volume 4—The Tale of a Turbine*. From this direct experience, Newton used a children's nursery rhyme to describe what he and his N&W colleagues simply called "The Locomotive." Recalling the little girl in a Henry Wadsworth Longfellow poem,

Newton said of the TE-1, "when she was good, she was very, very good. But when she was bad, she was horrid."[58]

Mr. Newton concludes his account of the TE-1 with this telling and heartfelt statement:

"If in the future someone should happen to have thoughts about attempting to develop a form of motive power utilizing coal as a power source, I suggest that arrangements be made to burn the coal in a stationary plant and transmit the power through wires to the locomotive—in other words electrification, eminently successful in many parts of the world.

"Another option may exist if petroleum prices go out of sight: Convert the coal to a liquid fuel for a diesel-electric locomotive. Until then, *Jawn Henry*, you did your best. May you rest in peace."[59]

3

Gas turbine locomotives and trains

The gas turbine locomotives and trains discussed in this chapter operated between 1948 and 2003. Gas turbine freight locomotives were expected to equal or exceed the performance of diesel-electric locomotives, while costing less to operate. Gas turbine passenger trains were expected to be cost-effective compared to diesels, but additionally they were expected to increase interest in passenger rail travel.

Advantages and disadvantages

These were the anticipated advantages of using gas turbines as railroad motive power:
- Greater power density—smaller, lighter for power output
- Wide variety of fuels
- Lower cost fuels
- Reduced or no cooling systems and coolant water
- Reduced maintenance
- Reduced lubrication requirements
- Smoother operation
- Lower overall cost to own and operate
- Capable of pulling heavier freight trains at higher speeds
- Substitute for electrification for high speed passenger service
- Fewer emissions

Reduced maintenance requirements were anticipated because gas turbines have far fewer moving parts than diesel engines, *i.e.* little more than a rotating compressor/turbine shaft plus fuel and lubricating pumps. However, reliability and maintenance were still issues for these locomotives and power cars. Typically, they required separate maintenance facilities and special training for maintenance staff, resulting in additional costs.

Weight reduction could cut both ways. While weight reduction is advantageous for passenger locomotives, freight locomotives must be heavy in order to effectively apply huge amounts of tractive effort to the rails.

Unfortunately, the gas turbine locomotives and trains discussed here had other weaknesses. Foremost among them was especially poor energy efficiency (fuel economy) when not operating at or near full speed and load. This, of course, undermined anticipated cost-saving. Some gas-turbine-powered locomotives were also noisy, producing a loud, high-pitched whine not appropriate for populated areas.

Additionally, while gas turbine locomotives and trains operating before the year 2000 did not have to comply with federal exhaust emissions regulations, they still produced a considerable amount of air pollution.

Smog-producing nitrogen oxides (NOx) emissions from gas turbines could have been reduced with water injection to produce cooler combustion temperatures. However, to accomplish this, these locomotives would have needed water tenders, appendages with costly infrastructures that the railroads gladly abandoned when diesel-electric locomotives replaced steam. Water injection had another major drawback: it lowered energy efficiency.

A more contemporary approach for reducing NOx emissions from gas turbines would be selective catalytic reduction (SCR), also known as urea aftertreatment. This technology passes exhaust gases and ammonia (in the form of urea-based exhaust fluid) over a catalyst, which is a substance that stimulates a chemical reaction without consuming itself. The chemical reaction looks like this:

$$NOx + Ammonia + SCR\ Catalyst \Rightarrow Nitrogen + Water$$

However, this technology is more easily applied to stationary gas turbines used in the power generation sector.

How gas turbines work

The gas turbine concept was first patented by Englishman John Barber in 1791. Of course, the original patented device looked little like modern gas turbines.

The operation of a contemporary simple cycle gas turbine can be described by these steps:

- Compression of inlet combustion air
- Injection of fuel into the compressed combustion air
- Ignition of the fuel/air mixture
- Expansion of hot combustion gases against curved turbine blades
- Production of shaft horsepower and output thrust

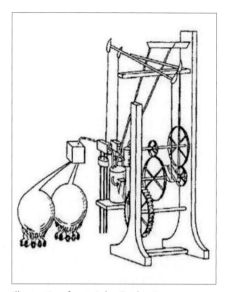

Illustration from John Barber's gas turbine British patent No. 1833 granted in 1791. The patent was titled "A Method for Rising Inflammable Air for the Purpose of Producing Motion and Facilitating Metallurgical Operations."
John Barber

A woman waves to the engineer in this 1953 Union Pacific publicity photo. The press release accompanying the photograph stated that it highlights motive power advances. The modern and powerful GTEL is contrasted with a 30-year-old electric car.
Union Pacific Railroad Museum

Like steam turbines, gas turbines are devices that convert thermal energy (heat) into mechanical energy. In the case of the gas turbine, the heat takes the form of highly pressurized gaseous combustion products. Unlike steam turbines, gas turbines are internal combustion engines because combustion of fuel takes place within the turbine engine itself. (The steam that rotates a steam turbine is produced externally by boiling water in a boiler.)

Because gas turbines are internal combustion engines, they are potentially more energy efficient than steam turbines. Gas turbines, however, are generally not more efficient than diesel engines.

Gas turbine engines take two forms:
- Jet engine
- Turboshaft engine

Jet engine gas turbines are designed to primarily produce exhaust thrust. This thrust creates propulsion and mechanical energy in the opposite direction of the exhaust, thus pushing the turbine and whatever is attached to it forward.

In contrast, turboshaft gas turbine engines are designed to minimize exhaust thrust and instead maximize the amount of energy from the turbine's spinning shaft. This mechanical energy is then used to perform mechanical work external to the turbine.[64]

Both the jet engine and turboshaft engine use mechanical energy captured by the turbine's spinning blades to turn the blades of the engine air compressors. This is an unavoidable parasitic load, which may consume as much as two-thirds of the energy produced by the turbine blades. Thus, most of the gas turbine's output is consumed by itself.

Turboshaft gas turbine engines were used in the gas turbine locomotives and trains discussed here with the exception of the New York Central jet-powered Budd rail car, which was uniquely powered by aircraft jet engines mounted to its roof.[65]

In greater detail, we can understand how a simple cycle turboshaft gas turbine engine works as follows:
- Combustion air is sucked into the air inlet of the engine by fan blades of a rotating compressor whose successive stages increasingly compress the air to increase its density
- This denser air—which is more oxygen-rich—is forced into the turbine's multiple combustion chambers, where it is combined with an atomized fuel
- Spark plugs initially ignite this fuel/air mixture, after which combustion within the combustion chambers becomes self-sustaining
- Hot combustion gases pass through the combustion chambers' restrictive outlets, expand, and push against the multiple rows of curved turbine blades
- The turbine blades rotate on center shafts producing shaft horsepower that turns the turbine's compressor and provides output power for other devices

While this characterizes a simple cycle, single-shaft turboshaft gas turbine engine, gas turbines may be configured in a variety of other ways, adding complexity to boost power output and efficiency.

For example, a regenerative cycle may be added to recover waste heat from the gas turbine's exhaust stream; an intercooler could be used to improve the efficiency of a multistage air compressor; multiple shafts may be incorporated to rotate separate compressor and turbine sections; and "reheat" may be added in the form of an additional set of combustors to produce thrust to rotate a second set of turbines. Gas turbines may be designed for power generation or use in aircraft.

In a direct-drive, turboshaft gas turbine locomotive, the turbine's output shaft is connected to a set of step-down reduction gears that are mechanically connected to the locomotive's drive wheels. In a GTEL, the reduction gears are connected to generators that produce electricity for electric traction motors.

Like steam turbine locomotives, gas turbine locomotives and trains could burn a variety of fuels, including Bunker C, diesel fuel, and kerosene. While powdered coal might have been an attractive gas turbine fuel for coal advocates, it was problematic because of the problem of coal ash and cinder erosion of turbine blades.

Gas turbine locomotive and train energy efficiency

While the gas turbine in the proposed 1948 Allis-Chalmers coal-fired GTEL discussed below was anticipated to have 24% maximum efficiency,[66] the real-life Bunker C-fired gas turbine in the 4,500 horsepower Union Pacific GTEL was reported to operate in the 13-17% range in 1952.[67]

This efficiency was under full-load design conditions. It could be argued that 13-17% efficiency (or, say, 11-14% at the rail) was at least better than the 7-8% best fuel-to-rail efficiency of conventional steam locomotives. But the real comparison should have been with diesel-electric locomotives of the time. These were described as having 22-23% overall design efficiencies (at the rail).[68]

Gas turbines are at their most efficient when operating at full speed and load; they lose efficiency rapidly when operating at lower speeds, part-load, or when idling. Thus, just like with steam turbine locomotives, gas turbine locomotives and trains are not especially well-suited to the "duty cycle" of typical locomotive operation, which includes changing speeds and loads as well as idling for significant periods of time. While it may be possible to operate gas turbines in locomotives efficiently, doing so poses built-in challenges.

Take, for example, a UP 4,500 horsepower GTEL, which was reported to consume 200 gallons of fuel an hour when just idling at no load.[69] This idling energy loss was much greater than that of steam or diesel-electric locomotives. Even if early diesel-electric locomotives consumed four times as much fuel idling than the modest three to five gallons per hour of contemporary diesel-electrics, early diesel idling fuel consumption would have been 1/10th that of the UP GTEL. Compensating for this inefficiency was Bunker C's lower cost than diesel fuel.

Improving gas turbine energy efficiency

Gas turbine efficiency (work energy output divided by fuel energy input)

A worker examines an initial compressor blade in the engine's multi-stage axial compressor during assembly of a Siemens SGT5-8000H gas turbine. The large blades in the foreground compress inlet air prior to the combustion section. Smaller blades at the rear of this assembly create rotation from the expanding air/fuel mixture after combustion. Precision machining and material strength are critical to efficient and long-lasting turbines. Design improvements that produce incremental gains in life expectancy and fuel economy are closely guarded trade secrets of the few manufacturers worldwide. *Siemens*

is a function of a number of factors, including:

- Inlet air temperature and density
- Compression ratio
- Combustion efficiency
- Turbine inlet temperature
- Component efficiencies (compressor, turbines, pumps, etc.)
- Exhaust heat recovery
- Speed and load
- Blade cleanliness and overall maintenance

All of these factors imply general strategies for improving gas turbine efficiency. For example, the efficiency of the compressor (in compressing air) and the turbine (in extracting useful energy) could be increased by improving air foil blade design, reducing turbulence, minimizing clearances and leakage, employing special coatings, and reducing the mechanical friction of rotating parts.

However, design trade-offs may be encountered. If efficiency improvement is sought by increasing the compression ratio through the use of additional compressor stages, the additional sets of blades may require more horsepower. That additional parasitic load would tend to reduce output and efficiency.

Hotter combustion temperatures produce a thermodynamic advantage (i.e. greater efficiency, more power), but they could also produce destructive metallurgical stress. Strategies for avoiding that include thermal barriers that protect turbine parts from higher temperatures, improved materials that are resistant to higher temperatures, and design elements that cool turbine components subject to higher temperatures (i.e. turbine combustion chambers, blades, and casings).

An energy regenerator or recuperator is a heat exchanger that captures waste heat from a gas turbine's exhaust and uses it to preheat combustion air, **1**. Hotter combustion air results in hotter combustion gases, boosting energy output by 25% or more without the use of additional fuel.

But it was difficult to incorporate this technology in gas turbine locomotives because of the size and weight of the heat exchangers. The proposed Allis-Chalmers coal-fired GTEL would have used a recuperator.[70] While a good strategy for boosting energy efficiency, higher combustion temperatures could result in increased NOx production.

The efficiency of gas turbines is

significantly affected by inlet (ambient) air temperature. For example, the 4,500 horsepower UP GTEL was reported to lose 300 horsepower (7%) for every 10°F increase in ambient temperature.[71]

Less severe, though still significant, was the projected 20% horsepower loss for the Westinghouse "Blue Goose" GTEL gas turbine if ambient temperature increased 70°F from 10°F to 80°F.[72] While outside temperature is a given, supplied by the natural environment, there are circumstances when relatively cooler air can be found.

When operating in tunnels, for instance, it is possible to lower inlet air temperature by drawing combustion air from as close to the rails as possible. This practice would also maintain power output, the primary concern of railroads when operating in tunnels.

Because gas turbines operate much more efficiently at higher speeds and loads, it would have made energy sense to utilize these locomotives and trains on routes where these conditions can be maximized.

Uncongested dedicated passenger routes would serve Amtrak gas turbine trains well. The kind of long-distance transcontinental freight-hauling Union Pacific is known for could also fit that bill. However, since air pressure and therefore altitude is contraindicated for gas turbine energy efficiency, it also would have made energy sense to restrict these locomotives to lower altitudes—thus avoiding the Rocky Mountains—an impossible strategy for Union Pacific.

Noteworthy examples

The nine gas turbine locomotives and trains described in this chapter are presented in chronological order based on the date of construction of the first locomotive or train of their classes. Here again, unless noted otherwise, horsepower ratings represent turbine power output, not power delivered to generators or the rail. These locomotives and trains were an interesting and varied lot.

The first gas turbine locomotive discussed here is GE's second attempt to build a turbine locomotive that operated on inexpensive Bunker C fuel oil. However, unlike GE's previously discussed unsuccessful Bunker C fuel oil-fired STEL, this gas turbine electric locomotive was a success.

Union Pacific purchased a fleet of these Bunker C fuel oil-fired GTELs and they operated in heavy freight service for more than two decades (1948-1970). While performance dropped off as they aged, out of the box these locomotives averaged 10,000 miles a month with an availability greater than 80%.[74]

Shortly after the introduction of this GE GTEL, Westinghouse-Baldwin attempted to enter the Bunker C-GTEL market, but did so unsuccessfully with its "Blue Goose" locomotive (1950-1953). Union Pacific then built a coal-fired GTEL that didn't work well enough to use or replicate (1962-1964).

These efforts were followed by the New York Central Jet Car (1966) and gas turbine passenger trains, including the Long Island Railroad's gas turbine commuter test cars (1966-1977) and Amtrak TurboTrains and Turboliners (1968-2003), the latter operating successfully for a number of years.

A powerful natural gas-fired gas turbine locomotive, the Compressed Integrated Natural Gas Locomotive (CINGL), was proposed but not built (1994-1997), followed by the intriguing high-speed Bombardier JetTrain prototype that Amtrak decided not to purchase (2000-2002).

The sidebar "The Fastest Turbine-Powered Locomotive and Train" on page 110 recognizes the world's fastest gas turbine locomotive, the French Alstom-built TGV No. 001 (1972-1978).

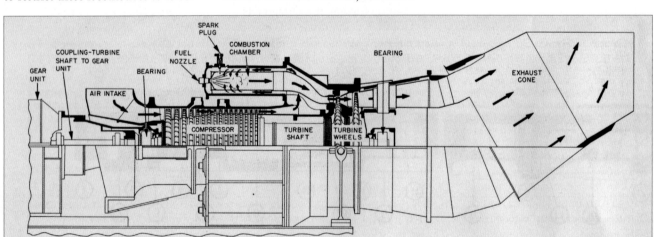

This cutaway diagram shows the inside workings of General Electric 8,500 horsepower Bunker C fuel oil-fired, turboshaft engine used in the more powerful second generation Union Pacific GTELs. Visible, from left to right, are the air inlet, a multi-stage axial air compressor, one of the engine's combustion chambers, two turbine rotors, and the exhaust outlet. A single shaft connects the turbine rotors, the compressor rotors, and electrical generators. The latter (not pictured but connected to the gear unit at the far left of the illustration) supplied electricity to the locomotive's traction motors. *Union Pacific Railroad Museum*

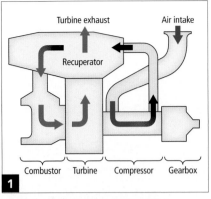

1

A recuperator improves the efficiency of a gas turbine engine. Cool intake air enters the inlet opening and then travels to the air compressor where it is compressed and heated. After compression this combustion air passes through the recuperator where it receives additional heat from turbine exhaust gases. The hot, compressed air is then combined with fuel and combusted, turning turbine blades before exiting from the engine as turbine exhaust.

How gas turbine power plants achieve higher levels of efficiency

Like steam turbine systems, the overall energy efficiency of turboshaft gas turbine systems can be vastly improved by utilizing a "combined cycle" to recover exhaust heat energy that would be otherwise wasted to the atmosphere by the primary turbine. A recuperator would recover some of this energy as would a combined-cycle gas turbine system. In such a system, hot gas turbine exhaust passes through a steam generator before being exhausted. The steam produced is then used to turn a steam turbine. Thus, a gas turbine combined cycle involves the use of both gas and steam turbines—the top and bottom cycles, respectively.

A steam generator is another name for a type of gas-to-liquid heat exchanger. Water is pumped through the heat exchanger in finned pipes exposed to the hot exhaust gases that are typically well over 500°F. As the heat is transferred across the pipe's finned surface area, the water is heated quickly and flashes to steam, which is then directed against turbine blades to rotate the steam turbine. With this second turbine generating additional electricity, a higher overall energy efficiency is achieved.

Combined-cycle gas turbine systems in stationary power plants can now produce overall thermal efficiencies of 60% or more without counting non-electrical energy use.[73]

However, combined-cycle gas turbine systems were not utilized in GTELs for many reasons: cost, complexity, reliability, space constraints, and weight. Another factor was the need for water to run the steam portion of the cycle. A functional condensing tender might have solved the water supply problem (by continuously recycling water), but tenders of this type would also be costly, complex, and yet another source of unreliability. Additionally, they would require a water infrastructure. Of course, the motive for looking for efficiency improvement was muted for gas turbines running on cheap fuel.

EXAMPLE 1: UNION PACIFIC FUEL OIL-FIRED GTEL

Gas turbine electric locomotives (GTEL)[75]

- 1948-1970
- 4,500-10,000 horsepower
- Bunker C fuel oil-fired
- 56 locomotives designed and built by GE and the American Locomotive Company. See roster, page 66
- Operated solely by Union Pacific Railroad

In 1948, GE and Alco rolled out an impressive fuel-oil burning prototype GTEL at GE's Erie, Pa., plant. The locomotive was slated for extensive testing on the Union Pacific RR.[76] Significantly, its 4,500 horsepower output was three times that of diesel-electric locomotives of the era. The railroad's evaluation of this locomotive led UP to purchase and receive 55 more gas turbine locomotives between 1951 and 1956, including some 10,000 horsepower units. Significantly, the 4,500 horsepower units could replace on a one-to-one basis UP's massive steam locomotive, the 4-8-8-4 Big Boy.

The initial test-bed and prototype was developed in 1947 and nick-named "Bessie." That name—short for "Messy Bessie"—was given to the locomotive after it suffered "one of its more spectacular" high-pressure leaks of Bunker C fuel oil inside the locomotive's carbody.[77]

This prototype was equipped with a 4,500 horsepower gas turbine engine with a 15-stage axial flow combustion air compressor, six combustion chambers, and two turbines that were connected to four electrical generators. The turbine's 6,900 rpm output was reduced by reduction gearing to 1,650

Union Pacific GTEL No. 29, probably Green River, Wyo. These locomotives were known for their large appetites, consuming about twice as much fuel as a similarly powerful diesel locomotive consist of the time. *Roger Puta*

The first gas turbine-electric locomotive (GTEL) in the United States rolled out of the General Electric Erie, Pa., shops in 1948. Its successful testing on the Union Pacific led to orders for 55 more GTELs. *General Electric*

rpm for the generators. The electrical output powered the locomotive's eight traction motors—one motor per axle in a four-truck B+B+B+B wheel arrangement—and auxiliary functions.

Bessie was a single unit locomotive with cabs on both ends. As such, it was unique among UP gas turbine locomotives, which otherwise had single cabs.

The turbine in this locomotive was started and stopped on diesel fuel. Shutting the turbine down on diesel fuel was necessary to clear all lines, filters, and nozzles of Bunker C fuel oil that otherwise would have cooled and congealed in these components, preventing the turbine from being restarted. Once running at 65% to 80% of full speed on diesel fuel, the switch to Bunker C fuel would occur.[78]

In order to use Bunker C, this highly viscous fuel was heated by heating coils located in the bottom of the Bunker C fuel tanks and in fuel lines just before the fuel filters. These filters cleaned the Bunker C prior to its injection into the turbine's combustion chambers. The heating coils were warmed by steam produced by a diesel fuel-burning steam generator. Bunker C was heated to 110°F in the fuel tank and 240°F before entering the combustors.[79] Using this cheap fuel was not easy!

Bessie's 4,500 horsepower turbine produced 3,800 horsepower at the rails and was said by GE test engineer David I. Smith to operate with a thermal efficiency as high as 17%.[80] This figure applies only to the efficiency of the gas turbine itself. But what about fuel-to-rails efficiency?

From the information provided above, we can calculate the fuel-to-rails maximum efficiency of the locomotive as follows:

Locomotive fuel-to-rails efficiency = prime mover efficiency x electric transmission efficiency

Where "electric transmission efficiency" is roughly equal to the efficiency of the electrical generators and electric traction motors

Electric transmission efficiency
= 3,800 horsepower
÷ 4,500 horsepower = 0.84 or 84%

Therefore, maximum locomotive fuel-to-rails efficiency = 0.17 x 0.84
= 0.14 or 14%

Thus, for every 100 units of energy consumed by the locomotive, 14 units of

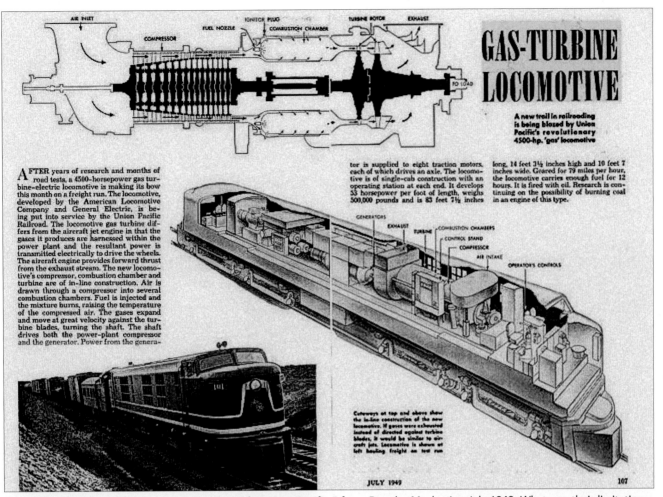

GAS-TURBINE LOCOMOTIVE

A new trail in railroading is being blazed by Union Pacific's revolutionary 4500-hp. 'gas' locomotive

AFTER years of research and months of road tests, a 4500-horsepower gas turbine-electric locomotive is making its bow this month on a freight run. The locomotive, developed by the American Locomotive Company and General Electric, is being put into service by the Union Pacific Railroad. The locomotive gas turbine differs from the aircraft jet engine in that the gases it produces are harnessed within the power plant and the resultant power is transmitted electrically to drive the wheels. The aircraft engine provides forward thrust from the exhaust stream. The new locomotive's compressor, combustion chamber and turbine are of in-line construction. Air is drawn through a compressor into several combustion chambers. Fuel is injected and the mixture burns, raising the temperature of the compressed air. The gases expand and move at great velocity against the turbine blades, turning the shaft. The shaft drives both the power-plant compressor and the generator. Power from the genera-

tor is supplied to eight traction motors, each of which drives an axle. The locomotive is of single-cab construction with an operating station at each end. It develops 53 horsepower per foot of length, weighs 500,000 pounds and is 83 feet 7½ inches long, 14 feet 3½ inches high and 10 feet 7 inches wide. Geared for 79 miles per hour, the locomotive carries enough fuel for 12 hours. It is fired with oil. Research is continuing on the possibility of burning coal in an engine of this type.

Cutaways at top and above show the in-line construction of the new locomotive. If gases were exhausted instead of directed against turbine blades, it would be similar to aircraft jets. Locomotive is shown at left hauling freight on test run

JULY 1949   107

A look inside "Bessie," the first GE GTEL slated for Union Pacific," from *Popular Mechanics*, July 1949. Whatever their limitations and failings, these locomotives hauled a lot of freight and were fascinating to railroaders, railfans, and those just technically inclined. *Popular Mechanics*

The gas turbine engine for General Electric's experimental locomotive is bolted to its test stand in Schenectady, N.Y., in 1948. *General Electric*

Giants meet in 1956 at the Cheyenne, Wyo, station—a UP 4-8-8-4 "Big Boy" steam locomotive and a super turbine. The super turbines produced nearly double the horsepower of the Big Boys. *Union Pacific Railroad Museum/David P. Oroszi collection*

energy or useful work are produced. The use of "maximum" above is important to note because gas turbine efficiency dropped significantly when operating at less-than-optimal full-load conditions.

A central challenge in designing and building the UP GTELs was adapting large gas turbine engines to the harsh conditions of railroad operation where locomotives are subject to strong impacts with frequent starts, stops, and changing loads.

Aside from the turbine engine issues, Bessie's development history is rife with interesting stories of component failure.[81] For example, combustion was initiated in turbine combustion chambers by retractable spark plugs. When these failed to retract, they melted in place.

If steam pressure dropped below fuel pressure in the Bunker C heating coils, the Bunker C would leak into the steam side of the steam coils and then into steam lines, leaving these almost impossible to clean.

More catastrophically, the gas turbine itself once exploded on a test stand at GE's locomotive plant in Erie, Pa. Some turbine parts flew long distances out of the plant into an adjacent neighborhood. While terrible to the victim, fortunately there was only one serious injury.

Between 1948 and 1951, Bessie was tested on all of UP's main routes, covering 101,231 miles,[82] and was required to accept freight trains whenever the locomotive was available and motive power was needed.

This aggressive and thorough testing regime convinced UP to purchase 10 more 4,500 horsepower gas turbines from GE in 1951, 15 more 4,500

horsepower turbines in 1953, and 30 8,500 horsepower gas turbines in 1955 and 1956, with some upgraded to 10,000 horsepower.

The 4,500 horsepower locomotives were over 80 feet long, weighed 551,000 pounds, and were capable of 137,930 pounds of starting tractive effort.[83] They arrived as single units with built-in diesel fuel and Bunker C fuel tanks. They were later equipped with separate tenders for Bunker C fuel.

In addition to a gas turbine engine, the 4,500 horsepower units were equipped with a 250 horsepower diesel engine. It was used to bring the turbine up to speed for starting and to run auxiliaries, provide excitation current to traction motors for dynamic braking, and move the locomotive around the yard when the turbine was off.

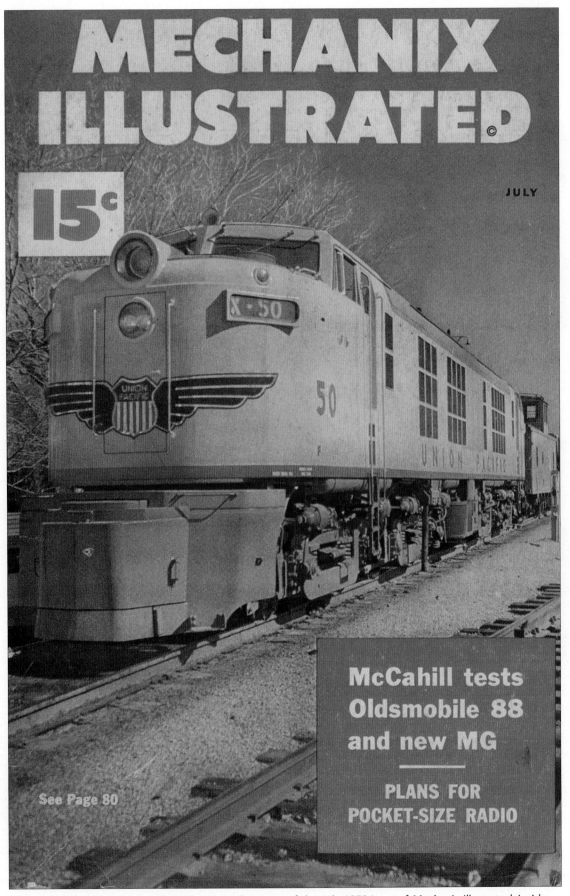

MECHANIX ILLUSTRATED ©

15¢

JULY

X-50

UNION PACIFIC

50

UNION PACIFIC

See Page 80

McCahill tests Oldsmobile 88 and new MG

PLANS FOR POCKET-SIZE RADIO

A dramatic photograph of a UP GTEL graces the cover of the July 1950 issue of *Mechanix Illustrated*. Inside were articles about the locomotive, road testing the new Oldsmobile 88, and how to build a rowboat, ice chest, wading pool, and mini radio. *Mechanix Illustrated*

First-generation 4,500 horsepower gas turbine locomotive No. 51 was the first production model. These locomotives initially used heated onboard Bunker C fuel tanks. The 7,200-gallon tanks gave the locomotives an approximate range of 400 miles. They were later equipped with heated fuel tenders. *David P. Oroszi collection*

Number 18, one of only two remaining UP super turbines, is preserved at the Illinois Railroad Museum. This two-unit locomotive was rated at 10,000 horsepower and equipped with a 24,000 gallon tender. Signs at the museum note the tender was originally used by a UP 4-8-4 steam locomotive and was rebuilt with electric heating elements to allow Bunker C fuel oil to flow at 200°F. Maximum fuel consumption for turbine No. 18 is given at 800 gallons per hour. *Walter Simpson*

A Union Pacific 8,500 horsepower "Super Turbine" at Dale, Wyo., heads toward Sherman Hill. The gas turbine engine is located in the locomotive's second unit. The third unit is the tender carrying up to 24,000 gallons of fuel oil, compared to 3,000 gallons for diesel-electric freight locomotives of the era. *Union Pacific Railroad Museum*

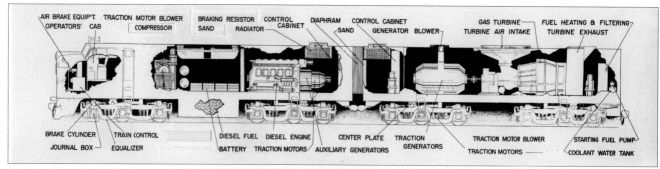

This cutaway view shows the components of the General Electric 8,500 horsepower gas turbine-electric. The front unit housed an 850 horsepower diesel engine for low-speed maneuvering. The turbine was in the rear unit. *General Electric*

The first 8,500 horsepower UP GTEL was put in mainline service on August 31, 1958.[84] The huge work potential of these "Super Turbines" was evident immediately. In September 1960, for example, the first 19 of these workhorses were hauling a remarkable 12.6% of Union Pacific's gross ton-miles of freight.[85] By 1964, they were averaging 116,000 miles a year, hauling nearly 16% of UP freight.[86]

The 8,500 and 10,000 horsepower locomotives were double units with the "A" unit consisting of the operator's cab, an 850 horsepower diesel engine (for the purposes just given), air compressor, and dynamic braking grids. The "B" unit carried the gas turbine and electrical generating equipment.

These turbine engines utilized compact positive displacement "Spiraxial" air compressors, which compressed air with two close clearance meshing rotors, and had 10 combustion chambers.[87] All of the 8,500 and 10,000 horsepower locomotives were equipped with insulated 24,000-gallon Bunker C fuel tenders.[88] The overall length of the locomotive unit coupled to the tender was 178 feet. The weight of the locomotive without the tender was 849,000 pounds. Starting tractive effort was 212,312 pounds.[89]

The Super Turbines were billed as "the most powerful locomotives ever built." Many decades later, they are still among the most powerful. Less complimentary was "Big Blow," the

name given them because of their jet plane-like sound.

While the noise compared to other locomotives may have been exaggerated, it was loud enough to get the locomotive banned in some localities. Union Pacific's turbines primarily operated between Council Bluffs, Iowa, and Green River, Wyo., a route with plenty of open space.

General Electric's Smith tells an interesting story about meeting UP specifications for the higher-horsepower gas turbine locomotives. According to Smith, UP specified to GE that the next batch of locomotives should deliver 7,000 drawbar horsepower at 7,000 feet.

Given losses in the locomotive's electric transmission, that meant the

Super turbine No. 8 is in Council Bluffs, Iowa, on Nov. 11, 1959. The overall length of the locomotive is 178 feet. *Lou Schmitz, Dan Dover Collection, Courtesy of David P. Oroszi*

A 4,500 horsepower UP GTEL "Veranda" (Nos. 61-75, so-called because of the external walkways) is depicted in a watercolor climbing over the Wasatch mountain range with a "hot fruit drag" loaded with cabbage, carrots, celery, tomatoes, spinach, and mandarins. The train is 20 miles outside of Ogden, Utah, destined for Chicago and points East. *Gil Bennett, collection of Dick Harley*

Union Pacific GTEL No. 16 drifts downhill trailing a string of UP and SP diesel locomotives and long freight train near Borie, Wyo. *Mike Schafer*

turbine would have to produce 8,400 horsepower. And in order to get that output at 7,000 feet, the turbine would have to produce over 10,000 horsepower at sea level.

To that amount, Smith explained, GE added a "fouling factor" and then over-designed the turbine so it would produce 13,500 horsepower. Smith says on a cold day in Schenectady, N.Y., (where the turbines were built), one tested out at nearly 15,000 horsepower. [90]

This progression can be taken a step further. Given that as much as two-thirds of the horsepower produced by the turbine portion of a gas turbine engine is consumed by its air compressor, those GTEL rotating turbine blades may have been producing 45,000 horsepower to be able to output 15,000 horsepower on that chilly day in Schenectady. It's no wonder these turbines had an appetite for Bunker C fuel oil.

While these GTELs primarily burned Bunker C, Union Pacific experimented with different fuel options because Bunker C was a dirty, abrasive fuel (full of contaminants) and had corrosive impacts on gas turbine blades and combustion chambers.

Union Pacific tried more refined No. 5 fuel oil, which was less damaging to turbine blades though still viscous enough to require heating to flow properly. [91] Union Pacific also experimented with clean-burning but more expensive propane to address the corrosion problem. [92]

Not surprisingly, testing with propane showed that it burned cleaner, was non-corrosive, minimized blade and combustor maintenance, and eliminated fuel pump and filter problems, though fuel delivery took longer. Union Pacific's fuel of choice ended up being a specially refined version of Bunker C subject to a de-salting wash prepared for UP by Richfield Oil. [93]

In the energy conservation field, it's axiomatic that low cost energy encourages and produces energy waste. The GTEL's generous consumption of cheap fuel oil exemplified this principle. The efficiency of these giant GTELs was described as half that of a diesel-electric locomotive of the time. While Smith generously assigned a maximum efficiency of 17% to Bessie's gas turbine engine, information provided in Thomas Lee's *Turbines Westward* suggests a slightly lower

maximum turbine efficiency.

At full throttle, Lee reports that the 4,500 horsepower UP GTELs consumed 600 gallons of fuel per hour. [94] From this information, turbine efficiency can be calculated as follows:

1 gallon of Bunker C fuel oil
= 150,000 BTUs

Turbine energy input
= 600 gal/hr x 150,000 BTUs/gal
= 90,000,000 BTUs/hr

1 horsepower-hour = 2,545 BTUs

4,500 horsepower output
= 4,500 hp-hr/hr

Turbine energy output
= 4,500 hp-hrs/hr x 2,545 BTUs/hp-hr =
11,452,500 BTUs/hr

$$\text{Energy efficiency} = \frac{\text{energy output}}{\text{energy input}}$$

$$\frac{11,452,500 \text{ BTUs/hr}}{90,000,000 \text{ BTUs/hr}}$$
= 0.127, or 12.7%, say 13%

UP Big Blow No. 4 is at Evanston, Wyo., on March 11, 1962. Close inspection reveals that this 8,500 horsepower turbine is followed by six 1,750 horsepower GP9s for a total of 19,000 horsepower. It's unlikely that all this power could be used at low speeds because the tractive effort would likely break one of the couplers on the train. *Collection of Chris Zygmunt*

Elsewhere, it is reported that a 4,500 horsepower UP GTEL would consume its fuel tank of 6,600 gallons of Bunker C fuel oil in 12 hours at full output. That performance equates to a maximum gas turbine efficiency of 13.8% or 14%, with less efficiency at lower turbine speeds and loads.[95] It would be best to operate these gas turbines where they could run flat out, loaded up, climbing mountains, and free of terminal or traffic congestion.

As previously mentioned, all of UP's GTELs were equipped with smaller diesel engines. These allowed engineers to keep their locomotive's gas turbines off when their operation was unnecessary and would be most wasteful. For example, when going down long hills (an operation that did not require much horsepower), UP engineers would turn off gas turbines and run their locomotive and train auxiliaries on the locomotive's much more energy efficient auxiliary diesel engines.[96]

Union Pacific's operational policy also required that gas turbine engines not idle for more than 30 minutes.[97] The 4,500 horsepower gas turbines

Union Pacific No. 52 leads a freight train through Weber Canyon in the Wasatch mountain range near Ogden, Utah. This first-generation UP GTEL was equipped with a 4,500 horsepower gas turbine engine, which produced 137,930 pounds of starting tractive effort and 105,000 pounds of continuous tractive effort at 12.9 mph. Maximum speed was 65 mph. Its onboard fuel tanks carried 7,200 gallons of Bunker C fuel oil and 1,000 gallons of diesel fuel. *Union Pacific Railroad Museum*

consumed 200 gallons of Bunker C per hour when idling, a full 33% of the fuel consumed when they were producing full horsepower.[98] The higher horsepower gas turbines consumed and wasted proportionately more when idling.

One way of appreciating the colossal energy wastefulness of UP's GTELs is by considering the turbine engine's exhaust. At full output, the super turbines produced 850°F exhaust gas at the rate of 320,000 cubic feet per minute.[99] That exhaust—it might as well have been a giant flame thrower—contained enough energy to heat a small town on cold winter days.

General Electric was well aware that

By the late 1960s, other uses for Bunker C fuel were being found, causing the price to increase. This spelled the end for the fuel-hungry UP turbine locomotives like No. 12 in Granger, Wyo., in August 1968. *Richard Steinheimer*

The Intercontinental Engineering scrap yard in Riverside, Mo., became the graveyard for super turbines by 1976. *Allen Rider*

A turbine engine's combustors and vertical exhaust duct, left, are evident in this photo. *Allen Rider*

its inefficient though powerful GTELs were cost-effective only because of the price differential between Bunker C fuel oil and diesel fuel. It also knew that a favorable differential could not be guaranteed.

By the late 1960s, refinery operations changed and other purposes (e.g. manufacture of plastics) were found for Bunker C. With greater demand for this fuel, its price went up. A price increase of just pennies on the gallon, combined with a growing list of costly maintenance issues, ended this GTEL's motive power reign.

The maintenance issues included problems with pumps, nozzles, heating equipment, and ongoing corrosion of turbine blades by the Bunker C fuel. Additionally, dirt and dust fouled compressor stages. When filtration was increased to reduce that fouling, the gas turbine's limited efficiency was further reduced.[100]

Union Pacific GTEL roster					
Built	Road number	Builder	Horsepower	Retired	Notes
1948	50	Alco-GE	4,500	1951	1
1952	51-56	GE	4,500	1962	
1953	57-60	GE	4,500	1962 (57), 1963 (60), 1964 (58, 59)	
1954	61-75	GE	4,500	1963 (61-66, 71-73, 75), 1964 (67-70, 74)	2
1958	1-5	GE	8,500	1968 (1-4), 1969 (5)	
1959	6-11	GE	8,500	1969 (6, 9-11), 1970 (7, 8)	
1960	12-24	GE	8,500	1968 (19), 1969 (12, 13, 15, 17, 20, 24), 1970 (14, 16, 18, 21-23)	
1961	25-30	GE	8,500	1969 (25), 1970 (26-30)	
Notes:					
1. Dual cab demonstrator owned by General Electric					
2. Veranda style with side walkways					

UP Super Turbines await recycling

This photo shows more clearly six of the engine's 10 combustors along with the air compressor and air intake. *Allen Rider*

A GTEL's control stand is exposed to the elements. *Allen Rider*

GE ignores market for smaller GTELs

Once GE knew that its 4,500 horsepower GTEL was successful with Union Pacific, the locomotive manufacturer hired consulting engineering firm Gibbs & Hill to study what GE needed to do in order to attract a larger market for gas turbine locomotives.[101] In a report dated March 27,1953, Gibbs & Hill concluded that:

• GE could sell more flexible 4-axle 2,500 horsepower gas turbine units than it could higher horsepower units, i.e. 270 2,500 horsepower units compared to 50 4,500 horsepower units annually by 1965.[102]

• In the years ahead, GTELs would probably consume diesel fuel for some portion of their operating hours because a steady supply of sufficiently inexpensive Bunker C fuel would not likely be available.[103]

• Coal should not be considered a viable gas turbine fuel.[104]

• GE's low-efficiency design concept should be abandoned in favor of the development of higher-efficiency gas turbines.[105]

Gibbs & Hill noted that the full-load energy efficiency of GE's then-current gas turbine engines was about 17.5%, while 24.5% efficiency would be needed[106] along with much better part-load efficiency. To achieve that level of performance, the consultant observed that these improvements would be needed:

• Design modifications to permit an increase in turbine inlet temperature to 1,500°F

• A regenerator heat exchanger of at least 50% effectiveness

• Improved machine efficiencies (to reduce friction)

The report also suggested consideration of an intercooler to cool combustion air between compression stages, mechanical drive instead of electric drive, and a "free piston" combustor.

GE did not follow up on these recommendations. Instead, it built 30 highly inefficient 8,500 and 10,000 horsepower GTELs for UP while maintaining interest in developing a coal-fired GTEL.

EXAMPLE 2: BLUE GOOSE FUEL OIL-FIRED GTEL

Gas turbine electric locomotive (GTEL)[107]

- 1950-1953
- 4,000 horsepower
- Bunker C fuel oil-fired (initially diesel fuel)
- A single locomotive designed and built by Westinghouse-Baldwin
- Tested on a number of railroads

In November 1947, Westinghouse and Baldwin decided to build a gas turbine electric locomotive that became known as the Blue Goose.[108] Two and a half years later, in April of 1950, the new GTEL was completed, and it entered road service in May of that year.[109] Its unusual name was derived from the unusual shape of its front end (reminiscent of Baldwin's "sharknose" diesel locomotives) and its paint livery—blue and gray with an orange-striped nose.

Initially operated on diesel fuel, this experimental Bunker C fuel oil-fired GTEL was Westinghouse-Baldwin's gambit to enter the GTEL market after the success of the GE-Alco GTEL was apparent at Union Pacific. Despite clever design features and successful testing, this bird did not take off. Additional copies were never manufactured for sale.

These three characteristics of gas turbines led Westinghouse to believe these engines could work well in locomotive service.[110]

- Gas turbines could produce more horsepower in the limited space of a

Baldwin-Westinghouse's Blue Goose arrives on time at Chicago & North Western's Madison Street Station in Chicago with train No. 514 on Oct. 20, 1952. The Blue Goose started a 90-day test period on the C&NW in September 1952 pulling Trains 511 and 514 between Chicago and Elroy, Wis. *Wallace W. Abbey*

Baldwins jockey for position at the Pittsburgh platform. The Blue Goose stands alone while a Baldwin "Centipede"diesel electric waits with a train. *From the collection of Johann Arthur Stamm*

locomotive than any other type of prime mover.

• With fewer moving parts, gas turbines could have exceptionally low maintenance expenses.

• Gas turbines appeared to have the potential to efficiently burn inexpensive fuels, perhaps even coal.

Westinghouse-Baldwin's GTEL was 77 feet, 11 inches in length, weighed 460,000 pounds, and was supported by four two-axle trucks. It could deliver 115,000 pounds of starting tractive effort and 52,800 pounds of continuous tractive effort.[111] This pulling power was equal to that of a two-unit diesel-electric passenger locomotive of that era, but it weighed only two-thirds as much and was half the length.[112]

The Blue Goose promised to provide fuel cost savings even though it consumed twice as much fuel as a comparable two-unit diesel-electric passenger locomotive.[113] Reportedly

a little "sluggish" on starting, the Blue Goose was said to perform well at speeds above 40 mph.[114]

While there were similarities, the Westinghouse-Baldwin locomotive differed in many ways from the GE-Alco UP GTEL:

• The Blue Goose was a 100-mph, heavy-duty passenger train locomotive.

• It was powered by two 2,000 horsepower gas turbines which had 23-stage axial flow compressors, 12 combustors, and eight-stage gas turbines.

• Through a single reduction gear, each gas turbine powered a "dual-armature" DC generator. This elongated type of generator had two traction armatures mounted in succession on the generator's shaft. Each armature served two traction motors in a single truck.[115]

• Auxiliary electrical needs were met

by two 50 kw DC generators mounted on extension shafts connected to the ends of the traction generators.[116]

• Two 2,500 pounds/hour boilers[117]—one heated by diesel fuel and the other by recovered heat from one of the turbine's exhaust—provided steam for:

  • Passenger car and locomotive space heating
  • Kitchen galley cooking
  • Bunker C fuel oil heating (100°F in the fuel tank and 240°F at the combustors' nozzles)[118]
  • Atomizing the fuel as it was injected into turbine combustors[119]

• A small 75 horsepower diesel engine was used for emergency battery charging and yard movements.

• The Blue Goose end trucks could move 2.5 inches laterally while its inner trucks could move 7.5 inches laterally in order to negotiate curved track.[120]

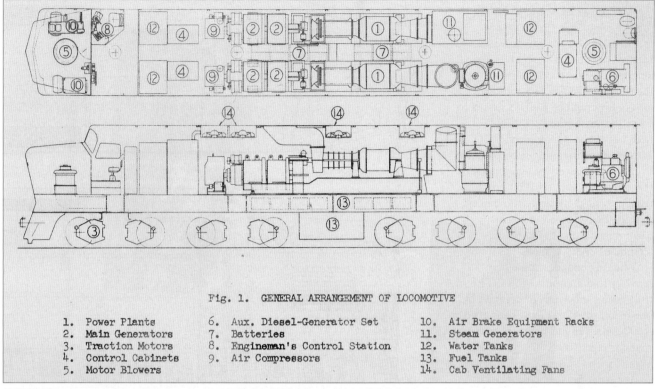

Fig. 1. GENERAL ARRANGEMENT OF LOCOMOTIVE

1. Power Plants	6. Aux. Diesel-Generator Set	10. Air Brake Equipment Racks
2. Main Generators	7. Batteries	11. Steam Generators
3. Traction Motors	8. Engineman's Control Station	12. Water Tanks
4. Control Cabinets	9. Air Compressors	13. Fuel Tanks
5. Motor Blowers		14. Cab Ventilating Fans

Blue Goose cutaway illustration showing components and layout. *Railway Mechanical and Electrical Engineer*

An engineer checks one of the Blue Goose's 2,000 horsepower gas turbines. Just to his left is the turbine's air intake. He is standing in front of the engine's axial compressor. To his right, under the housings, are the turbine engine's combustors, rotors, and exhaust duct. *From the collection of Johann Arthur Stamm*

- Turbine noise was reported not to be an issue.[121]

The Blue Goose's exhaust waste heat recovery boiler system was unique among gas turbine locomotives. In the winter, passenger cars and the locomotive could be partially heated by waste heat that otherwise would have been lost to the environment.

Moreover, using the steam produced by this heat recovery system to atomize the fuel as it was injected into turbine combustors led one analyst to remark that the Blue Goose was the first gas turbine locomotive to utilize a "combined cycle,"[122] modest as it was.

While a good idea, some heat recovery could not make this GTEL truly energy efficient. For example, by one report the Blue Goose consumed 3,600 gallons of fuel on a 409-mile round trip between Chicago and Elroy, Wis.[123]

The same trip (presumably with similar load) was accomplished by a comparable two-unit EMD diesel-electric locomotive burning 1,600 gallons of diesel fuel. Here, the Blue Goose consumed more than two times as much fuel. But with Bunker C priced at 4.8 cents a gallon and diesel fuel at 11 cents a gallon, it was marginally cheaper to operate the Blue Goose.[124]

In 1952, Westinghouse noted that the Blue Goose was consuming Bunker C fuel that was priced at 3.8 cents per gallon and higher while diesel fuel prices were 8.6 cents per gallon and higher.[125] While not guaranteed for future years, this price spread was favorable to fuel cost savings.

A review of the literature suggests that this Westinghouse GTEL didn't experience turbine blade corrosion and deposition problems associated with the use of Bunker C fuel, though Westinghouse apparently did experiment with various grades of residual fuel and tried centrifugal treatment and inhibitors to neutralize harmful ash.[126]

The Westinghouse-Baldwin prototype operated on the Chicago & North Western, Union Pacific, Pittsburgh & Lake Erie, Pennsylvania, and Missouri-Kansas-Texas railroads. Impressively, the locomotive is reported

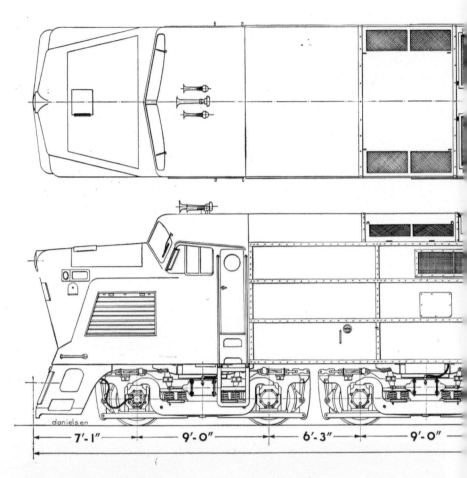

The Blue Goose pulls out of Pittsburgh Union Station with a test train. The 4,000 horsepower locomotive once pulled a 29-car passenger train from Altoona to Pittsburgh, Pa., unassisted. *From the collection of Johann Arthur Stamm*

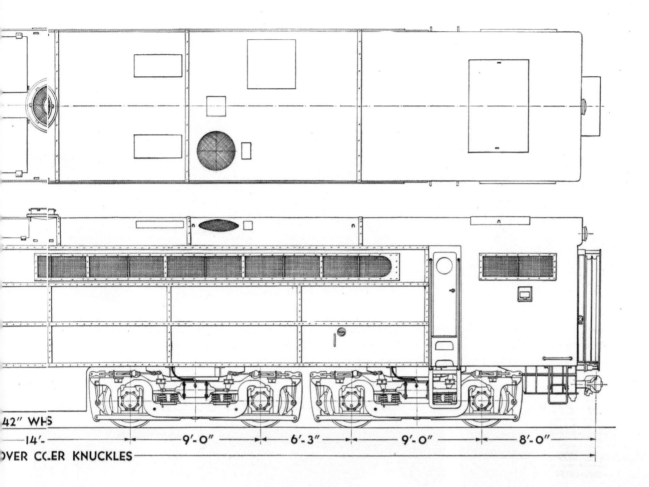

42" WHS

14'-

9'-0"   6'-3"   9'-0"   8'-0"

OVER COLER KNUCKLES

to have pulled up to 29 passenger cars on the mountainous route between Altoona and Pittsburgh, Pa.

While apparently performing competently, the Blue Goose completed testing just as Westinghouse was deciding to pull out of the locomotive business. As a result, none were sold and the prototype was dismantled in 1953.

This negative outcome stood in stark relief to early corporate enthusiasm for the locomotive and the expectation that it would operate in extended revenue service.[127] As previously intimated, Westinghouse even envisioned that a successful Blue Goose could have provided a gas turbine-powered return to the cheapest locomotive fuel—coal.[128]

The B-B+B-B gas-turbine-electric passenger locomotive, dubbed the "Blue Goose" because of its paint scheme (and perhaps for its unusual appearance), came just as builder Westinghouse was exiting the locomotive business. It was dismantled in 1953.
From the collection of Johann Arthur Stamm

This view of the Blue Goose's power plant shows the generator attached to the turbine. On the right is the gas turbine engine with air intake, compressor, and combustion chambers evident. On the left is the reduction gearing, dual-armature DC traction generator, and auxiliary generators shown as extensions to the traction generator. *Westinghouse Corporation*

Remembering a special encounter with the Blue Goose

Johann Arthur Stamm with the wooden model of the Blue Goose he built as a youth. *Walter Simpson*

Johann Arthur Stamm reviews Blue Goose blueprints at his home in suburban Pittsburgh, 70 years after his father, Johann Jacob Stamm, led the locomotive's testing effort for Westinghouse Corporation. *Walter Simpson*

Some of Johann Stamm's locomotive memorabilia. The locomotive builder's plate and bell had been presented to his father. *Walter Simpson*

Johann Arthur Stamm was 11 or 12 years old when his father took him to a Westinghouse Corporation open house in East Pittsburgh. It was the early 1950s and the Blue Goose gas turbine electric locomotive was on display.

Johann's father, Johann Jacob Stamm, was an electrical engineer who had worked for Baldwin Locomotive Works. In 1948, he left Baldwin and joined Westinghouse, soon becoming chief engineer responsible for testing the Blue Goose. His father's status made young Johann a special guest at the open house.

While other visitors could only walk through the locomotive's cab, Johann was taken by his dad on a special tour to see its inner workings. One turbine was running! And the sound was deafening!

Almost 70 years later, Johann remembers that experience as well as a Saturday trip with his father to the Union Switch and Signal repair shop where he saw the giant gears of the Blue Goose visible in an open gearbox that was being repaired. Another indelible memory of the son is how his dad had given his heart and soul to the Blue Goose and was "was never the same" after the project was scrapped.

Johann Jacob Stamm

The Baldwin-Westinghouse Blue Goose under construction in January 1950. The two auxiliary DC generators can be seen at the lower left just inside the roof opening. In this view looking toward the rear of the locomotive, the space for the second 2,000 horsepower turbine and generator set is taken by a table with sheets of blueprints spread on top. *Westinghouse Corporation*

UNION PACIFIC COAL-FIRED GTEL

Gas Turbine Electric Locomotive (GTEL)[129]

- 1962-1964
- 7,000 horsepower
- Pulverized coal-fired
- A single locomotive designed and built by Union Pacific
- Operated solely by UP

The UP coal-burning GTEL was a failed experiment. The railroad's desire for high horsepower through the use of low-cost fuel wasn't met with this 1962 gas turbine electric locomotive patched together from discarded locomotives and components. *Union Pacific*

Ever the leader in high-horsepower locomotive development, Union Pacific continued to experiment with gas turbines. In the early 1960s, UP shops constructed a monstrous 214-foot, three-unit, pulverized coal-burning GTEL. Potentially a prototype of UP's next generation of gas turbines, this locomotive was designed to burn UP-owned Wyoming coal supplies.[130]

The gas turbine's coal combustors and fly ash-removal and coal handling equipment were based on designs produced by the Locomotive Development Committee of Bituminous Coal Research Inc., a coal and railroad industry trade association. (See "The unsuccessful quest for a viable coal-burning GTEL" on page 78)

The coal-burning GTEL's three units consisted of:

- A rebuilt Alco PA passenger diesel locomotive that served as the locomotive's cab. It retained its 2,000 horsepower diesel engine and auxiliary equipment.

- A recycled Great Northern electric locomotive whose frame and trucks supported the coal combustors, fly ash filters, gas turbine, electrical generators, and an auxiliary diesel engine. The gas turbine used in this locomotive was formerly in a UP Bunker C fuel oil-fired GTEL. Eight of 12 axles on this second unit were equipped with electric traction motors.

- A tender formerly used by a UP 4-6-6-4 Challenger steam locomotive. This tender was modified to hold 61 tons of coal, presumably enough for 500 miles of freight hauling. It also contained an automatic coal handling system and a coal pulverizer.[131]

While this locomotive was a coal-burner (an environmental negative), it was also an excellent example of locomotive reuse and recycling.

Like UP's Big Blows, this coal-fired GTEL developed high horsepower. It was powered not only by the coal-fired gas turbine engine, now rated at 5,000 horsepower, but also by the Alco locomotive's original 2,000 horsepower diesel engine. The gas turbine was designed to initially run on diesel fuel before switching to pulverized coal. It had a total of 14 powered and four unpowered axles. The three-unit locomotive came in at 214 feet in length and 733,000 pounds. Its starting tractive effort was given as 127,275 pounds for the gas turbine unit and 60,832 pounds for the modified Alco PA unit.[132]

Union Pacific's coal-burning GTEL, however, racked up only 21,848 miles in revenue service, with only 488 hours under coal power.[133] Despite all the work imagining and assembling it, the locomotive was not a success and was not replicated.

Predictably, the turbine blade damage was worse with coal than with Bunker C fuel, even though the coal

was so minutely pulverized that it behaved as a fluid inside the turbine. A fly ash separator was used to clean up the combustor exhaust before it entered the turbine.

Unfortunately, the ash separator was not up to the task. Unconscionable by today's standards, the fine coal particles removed by the ash separator were released into the atmosphere in the turbine's exhaust stream.[134]

With less than 500 miles of coal-fired operation, inspection revealed that the combustor nozzles and turbine buckets were damaged by extensive corrosion. An earlier attempt by multiple parties to design and begin building a workable pulverized coal-burning GTEL had failed in large part for the same reason. This project is discussed on the following pages.

The lead unit of the coal-burning GTEL, shown in Council Bluffs, Iowa, in 1962, was a former Alco PA-1, which retained its 2,000 horsepower diesel engine. *Lou Schmitz*

The turbine section of the locomotive was built on a former Great Northern electric locomotive chassis. *Union Pacific*

The unsuccessful quest for a viable coal-burning GTEL[135]

Union Pacific's unsuccessful coal-fired GTEL experiment was preceded 15 years earlier by a multi-party endeavor to combine coal-burning and gas turbine technology in a locomotive. On January 12, 1945, a coal industry trade group known as Bituminous Coal Research Inc. (BCR) formed a Locomotive Development Committee (LDC) to explore the feasibility of creating a superior coal-burning locomotive able to compete against the diesel-electric locomotive with a strong emphasis on examining coal-fired gas turbine motive power.[136] In an era of post-World War II oil shortages, coal proponents thought that if technical hurdles were overcome, coal-burning gas turbine locomotives could become a popular form of motive power.[137] Bituminous Coal Research brought to the table a number of coal companies and railroads heavily invested in coal. This included the Baltimore & Ohio, Chesapeake & Ohio, New York Central, Norfolk & Western, Pennsylvania RR and the Virginian Ry.[138] By 1946, a reported 17 separate LDC projects were reported to be underway at six different institutions.[139] However, the effort was seen as misguided and futile by diesel locomotive manufacturer General Motors.[140]

In order to explore various ways coal could be burned by a gas turbine, the BCR's LDC examined these coal-based fuels:

- Finely powdered coal
- Synthetic gas produced on-board from coal
- Synthetic oil produced from coal "line-side," not on-board the locomotive[141]

The LDC selected the first option (a gas turbine burning pulverized coal) and focused its research on methods of pulverizing the coal, burning the coal in specially designed combustors, and removing fly ash from the gases escaping the combustors in order to protect the turbine blades from abrasion and erosion. The Locomotive Development Committee maintained that a coal-fired gas turbine would address the problem of "dwindling reserves of the known world oil deposits," producing a fuel bill only 50% of a diesel-electric locomotive's fuel bill and 33% of a conventional coal-burning steam locomotive's fuel bill.[142]

Allis-Chalmers, a company with extensive gas turbine experience, was one of two companies selected to develop the gas turbine concept for the LDC. The Allis-Chalmers proposal consisted of an approximately 4,000 horsepower Allis-Chalmers gas turbine driving four 1,000 horsepower electrical generators. It was hoped that 95% of the fly ash would be removed from the turbine's combustion gases by a battery of cyclone separators using centrifugal force to spin ash particles out of the combustion gas stream. The anticipated thermal efficiency of the turbine was 24%. This efficiency was to be achieved in large part by using a heat regenerator or recuperator heat exchanger (despite its size and weight) on the turbine's exhaust. The regenerator/recuperator was to be designed to recover 50% of the turbine's exhaust heat and put it to work preheating combustion air.

The LDC design of the turbine locomotive would have placed the turbine's combustion air inlet on the exterior of the locomotive in a manner designed to assist high speed aerodynamics—given the turbine's hunger for 100,000 cubic feet of air per minute.[143] By strategically aiming the inlet forward, the influx of combustion air might reduce aerodynamic turbulence or drag and perhaps even slightly pull the locomotive forward. Properly aiming the turbine's exhaust could also produce an aerodynamic benefit. While the LDC planned to purchase two coal-fired gas turbine locomotives by

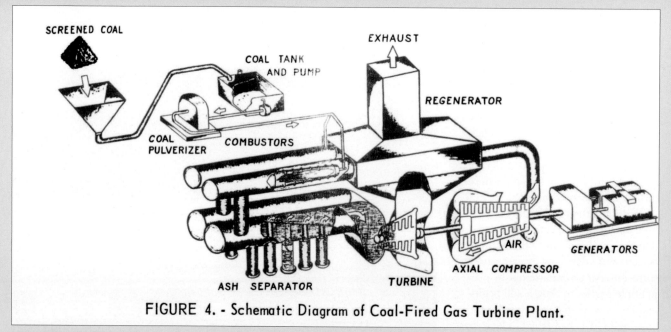

FIGURE 4. - Schematic Diagram of Coal-Fired Gas Turbine Plant.

This schematic diagram of a coal-fired gas turbine reveals the step-by-step process to produce electricity for locomotive traction motors. Beginning at the top left, the coal is pulverized and then combusted. The ash is then separated out before the exhaust from the combustion chambers strikes the turbine blades. The turbine shaft is connected to the engine's air compressor and the electrical generators. Note that before the turbine's exhaust is release into the atmosphere, it passes through a regenerator (also called a recuperator) where some of its heat is transferred to the combustion air. *U.S. Department of Mines*

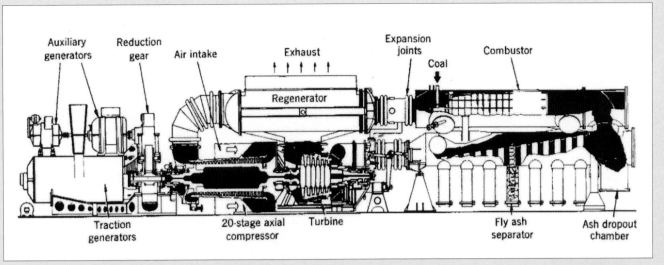

A cross-section of a proposed locomotive coal-fired gas turbine plant. *U.S. Department of Mines*

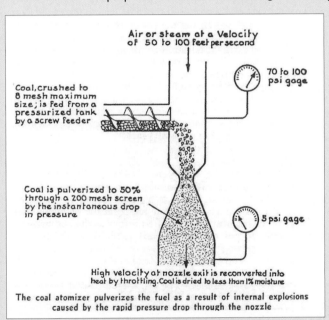

The coal atomizer pulverizes the fuel as a result of internal explosions caused by the rapid pressure drop through the nozzle

A coal pulverizer for a gas turbine. Coal would be pulverized by a pressurized air supply and nozzle that produced an instantaneous pressure drop, effectively pulling coal through the mesh. *Railway Mechanical Engineer*

Though Union Pacific's Bunker-C fuel oil turbine electric locomotives were successful, its experiment with a coal-fired version was less so. Extensive corrosion from the finely ground coal was revealed after less than 500 miles of use. *Chris Zygmunt*

1957, none were built and the project was canceled, citing "poor business conditions," presumably, for challenging diesels.[144]

However, the goal of building a viable coal-burning gas turbine locomotive persisted among coal interests. For example, in a 1961 paper, researchers at the federal Bureau of Mines' Coal Research Center in Morgantown, W.Va., revisited the work of the LDC.[145] They sought to solve the problem of coal ash erosion of turbine blades with newly designed turbine blades of Stellite,[146] and improved coal feeding methods. The paper was preliminary, without any discussion of results. Additionally, as mentioned on pages 76-77, Union Pacific used LDC designs for its 1962-1964 coal-fired GTEL, albeit unsuccessfully.

Interest in building coal-fired gas turbine locomotives surfaced again in the aftermath of the energy crises of 1973 and 1979 when oil supplies were constrained and oil prices rose significantly.[147] During this period, a number of reports and technical articles on coal-fired locomotives continued to be written under the auspices of the U.S. Department of Energy. A 1986 report, prepared by GE, whose interest in this type of locomotive spanned decades,[148] was titled "Economic Assessment of Coal Burning Locomotives."[149] Here, GE assessed the viability of three coal-fired gas turbine locomotives options:

- Coal slurry direct burning gas turbine
- Coal slurry direct burning gas turbine with steam injection
- Gasified coal burning gas turbine with steam injection
- Fluidized bed[150] coal-fired steam turbine

Additionally, the same report assessed:

- Coal slurry-fired diesel engine

According to the report, the coal slurry fuel GE evaluated would be a 50/50 mixture of fine coal particles and water. The gas turbine locomotive burning this fuel would have produced 5,900 horsepower and, according to GE, achieved a peak efficiency of 35% with what probably was an optimistic duty cycle or overall operating efficiency of 29%. In its report, GE explained that the locomotive would use two-spooling turbine technology[151] to improve part-load efficiency.

Of course, combusting fuel that's 50% water would produce a lot of steam. Because of water's significant latent heat of vaporization, recovering steam could produce a big efficiency boost. For this reason, GE proposed, as one of its locomotive options, the direct combustion of the slurry mix accompanied by capture and re-injection of the exhaust steam into the turbine as a form of waste heat recovery. This option, according to GE, would have boosted output to 8,000 horsepower, while raising peak turbine efficiency to 40% and duty cycle efficiency to a remarkable (and, again, perhaps optimistic) 34%.

While GE assigned a positive outlook to both versions of its theoretical coal slurry direct burning gas turbine locomotive (i.e. with and without steam re-injection), the company was less sanguine about the gas turbine option utilizing coal gasification with steam injection. In any event, this study was academic because fortunately none of the proposed coal-fired locomotives were ever built.

Coal is the most carbon-intensive fossil fuel, and when burned emits more carbon dioxide into the atmosphere per unit of energy released than oil or natural gas. It's now apparent that coal, in the absence of expensive and impractical carbon capture and sequestration, is an energy resource of the past because of the urgent need to reduce carbon dioxide emissions that contribute to climate change. The Intergovernmental Panel on Climate Change's 2018 assessment stated that the nations of the world must take unprecedented action by 2030 to avoid the risk of extreme drought, heat waves, wildfires, hurricanes, floods, and food shortages affecting hundreds of millions of people. Under these circumstances, ever revisiting the idea of using coal as a locomotive fuel wouldn't make sense.

The railroad industry will not return to coal-burning

"To insist that the railroads invest their money in coal-fired steam locomotives, which were recognized obsolete 10 years ago, is like asking the automobile companies, because of the shortage of steel and fuel, to return to the manufacture of carriages and wagons. That cannot happen and will not happen, nor will it happen to the railroad industry, regardless of the temporary pressures which may be brought to bear upon it."

—*Electro-Motive Division, General Motors Company*
September 25, 1948

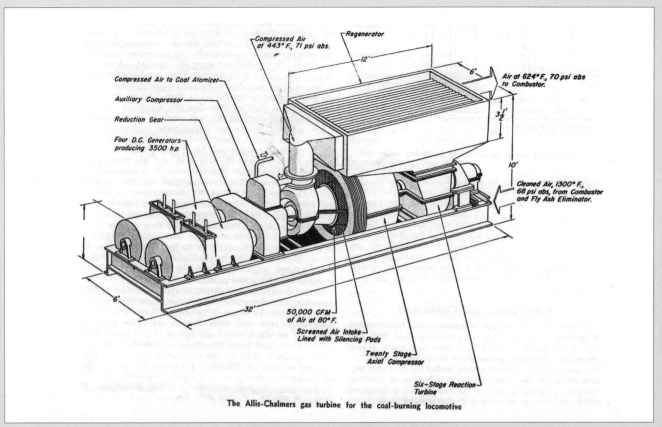

The proposed Allis-Chalmers coal-fired gas turbine engine with a large regenerator mounted to top of the compressor and turbine sections. *Railway Mechanical Engineer (November 1946)*

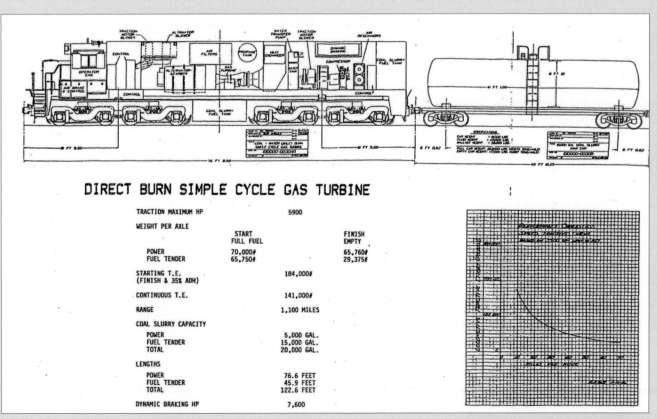

A 1986 General Electric report gives locomotive layout, specs, and tractive effort for direct-burning, coal slurry-fired gas turbine locomotives. *U.S. Department of Energy*

EXAMPLE 4: NEW YORK CENTRAL M-497 JET CAR

New York Central's M-497 is ready to run. The original design had the jet engines mounted on the rear roof section. The switch to the front roof mount was made to improve the looks of the M-497. This location, accompanied by canting the engines down five degrees, also helped keep the jet car more firmly on the tracks. Locomotive engineer Don Wetzel has denied rumors that the car became airborne. *Donald C. Wetzel Collection*

Jet engine gas turbine locomotive[152]

- 1966
- 10,000+ horsepower
- Kerosene-fueled
- A single test vehicle originally built by the Budd Company and then modified by the New York Central Railroad
- Operated solely by New York Central Railroad (NYC)

On July 23, 1966, New York Central Railroad's M-497 jet engine-powered, Budd-built former Rail Diesel Car (RDC) was timed at 183.85 mph along a 21-mile straight stretch of track between Butler, Ind., and Stryker, Ohio. This run set a U.S. passenger rail speed record that still stands today and was recognized as recently as 2011 in the Guinness Book of World Records.

The jet-powered Budd car was the creation of NYC's Technical Research Department, which was charged with the responsibility of determining the feasibility of operating high-speed rail vehicles on conventional, unimproved track and roadbed using state-of-the-art instrumentation available at the time.

Donald C. Wetzel, assistant to the director of technical research, led the effort under the direction of James J. Wright. Overall, more than 75 NYC

employees were involved. Wetzel was both a promoted locomotive engineer (who, ironically, was among the last to qualify on steam locomotives) and a bomber pilot. He was knowledgeable in jet engine technology, an important consideration because the M-497 would be powered by jet engines.

The Budd car used in this project was originally a 13-year-old stainless-steel-bodied, self-propelled RDC. While in NYC commuter service, the car was numbered M-497, and it kept that number as the jet-powered Budd.

In an unusual move, two jet engines were attached to the roof of the M-497 in order to quickly provide the test vehicle with 10,000+ horsepower. The GE J-47-19 jet engines, each rated at 5,200 pounds of thrust, were purchased surplus. They had originally been mounted under the wings of a U.S. Air Force B-36 bomber. The engines

The M-497 blasts through Bryan, Ohio, on July 23, 1966. On its second run, it set a 183.85 mph record. Ten-thousand horsepower rocketed the M-497 forward, while braking was accomplished by aerodynamic drag to 120 mph and then through the use of the Budd car's disk brakes to 50 mph. At that point, Wetzel let the brakes cool off before a final application to bring the M-497 to a stop. *New York Central*

On piloting the M-497

"Briefly flashing through my head were maintaining the throttle settings, observing the instruments, glancing outside, thinking that I had the crew's lives, AND, not in the least, President Perlman's life, in my hands. Coming to a facing point switch was sobering.

"I put my head down and hoped Chuck Popma had spiked it shut securely. Seeing a 4 x 8 sheet of plywood across the track—and not knowing what it was, was also a scary moment.

"Bob Kern, flying the chase plane, had radioed me about it, but I couldn't do anything but ride it out and worry, again, briefly. Later, the crew cut off the horn cord and gave it to me because they said I never let go of it."

—*Don Wetzel, October 9, 2018*

Engineer/pilot Don Wetzel stands in front of the record-setting M-497 Jet Car. Don was chosen to "pilot" M-497 because of his diverse experience as a locomotive engineer and aircraft pilot and his familiarity with jet engines. Don started taking flying lessons when he was 14 and continued those while in the Marine Corps. He joined the New York Central in 1950 as a locomotive fireman, later becoming a locomotive engineer, and was one of the last to operate the Central's steam locomotives. New York Central had a converted B-25 bomber for which Don was its chief pilot. *Donald C. Wetzel collection*

In the official "builder's photo," the NYC Collingwood, Ohio, Technical Center staff poses in front of its jet-powered creation. *Donald C. Wetzel collection*

An RB-36H bomber of the 72nd Strategic Reconnaissance Squadron flies over San Francisco Bay in 1954. The jet engines on the tips of the B-36 were the type used by the NYC Jet Car. *US Air Force*

were modified to operate on diesel fuel. Kerosene was used on the test runs.[153]

An angled "shovel-nosed" faring was installed on the front of the car for aerodynamics reasons and at the insistence of Ruth Wetzel, a commercial artist and the wife of Don Wetzel.

The signature nose was similar in shape to the front end of the 1934 Burlington *Zephyr*. Once painted dark gray, it earned the M-497 the nickname "Black Beetle," which was not at all popular with the shop and crew.

While Ruth Wetzel had initially sketched the nose on her sketch pad, the final shape was the product of wind tunnel testing at Case Western Reserve University in Cleveland.

The test car was significantly modified for this experiment. Due to anticipated high speeds, the transmission drive shafts of the Budd's two Detroit Diesel engines were disconnected from the axles, although the engines would be still be running during the tests to provide electrical power for onboard instrumentation and compressed air for braking.

Some passenger section seating was removed to allow for bracing of the jet engine mount. Scientific instrumentation was installed and connected to more than 50 sensors to measure speed, stress forces, bearing temperatures, ride characteristics, and other metrics.

A heat shield had to be installed on the roof to protect the diesel engines' radiator system from the jet exhaust. The wheels were also changed from those with tapered treads to cylindrical ones in the hope that such a modification would reduce "hunting" and improve high speed tracking. Hunting is the lateral (side-to-side) oscillation of railcar wheelsets between inside rail surfaces.

Test runs took place along a 68.5-mile formerly four-track (now two) main line tangent (straight track) right-of-way that stretches from Butler, Ind., to Air Line Junction, Ohio, west of Toledo. At the time of the test, most of the line was conventional 26-year-old, 127-pound jointed rail in 39-foot sections with some welded rail.

Train speed, track deflection, and other ground measurements were taken near the operations center in Bryan, Ohio. Significantly, Wetzel reported that his onboard speedometer, which previously had been tested for accuracy, showed 196 mph before he slowed down while traveling through the speed traps.[154] Wetzel recently said the M-497 probably had enough power to reach 220 mph.[155]

New York Central President Alfred E. Perlman joined Wetzel and his crew on the record run. Perlman served as "co-pilot" and was a strong supporter of the project. Costs were later given as $30,000 to $35,000, but Wetzel reports they were somewhat higher.

Don Wetzel shares some of the reactions to piloting the M-497 in "On piloting the M-497" on page 83. Here he refers to a facing point, which is the moving rail portion of a switch track that faces traffic.

He mentions Chuck Popma, who was NYC's vice president for engineering. Chuck was directly involved in the project making sure the trackage was safe for the high-speed

New York Central's idea of a snow blower. After the high-speed tests were complete, the ever-inventive NYC Technical Research Center installed one of the M-497's jet engines in a former caboose to create a snow blower used to clear snow and ice from yards. *Donald C. Wetzel collection*

test runs. Reference is also made to a 4 x 8 sheet of plywood that someone placed on the track and that Don could not avoid hitting. These runs took a lot of bravery.

While some doubted the serious nature of the experiment, probably because of M-497's unusual source of motive power in these tests (the two roof-mounted jet engines), NYC participants knew first-hand about the data collection and analysis that occurred during and after the

successful test runs. Two volumes of comprehensive test data were published afterward.[156]

The M-497 jet-powered Budd rail car was never intended to be a prototype railcar. Once the tests were over, it was remodeled back to its original condition and returned to its previous use. Ever-inventive, Wetzel turned the jet engines into snow blowing equipment for the NYC. This equipment was awarded U.S. and foreign patents.

MTA GAS TURBINE COMMUTER CARS

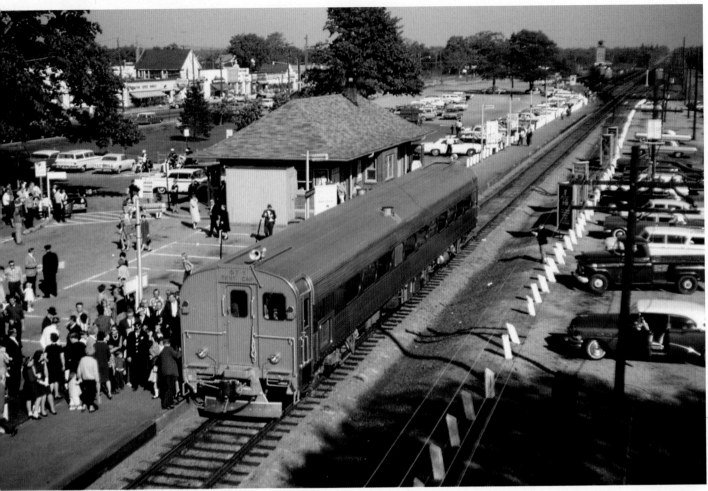

The public was invited by the Long Island Rail Road to see the initial run of the GT-1 gas turbine car at the Ronkonkoma, N.Y., station, on Sept. 12, 1966. Free rides were offered to the public from this station to Central Islip and back on Oct. 9, 1966. The Long Island Rail Road reported that 1,020 people turned out to ride. On that special day, 1,068 sodas, 500 coffees, and 480 donuts were distributed. *David Keller Archive*

Torque converter and gas turbine electric cars/trains[157]

- 1966-1977
- Diesel fuel-powered
- Two experimental cars and two experimental trains built by Budd, Garrett, and General Electric companies
- Operated solely on the Long Island Rail Road (LIRR) by the New York Metropolitan Transportation Authority (MTA)

An LIRR four-car GT/E commuter train passes Kings Parks State Hospital, on Nov. 11, 1977. The turbine vents at the top of the second car indicates this is a train of Garrett GT/E cars. *David Keller Archive*

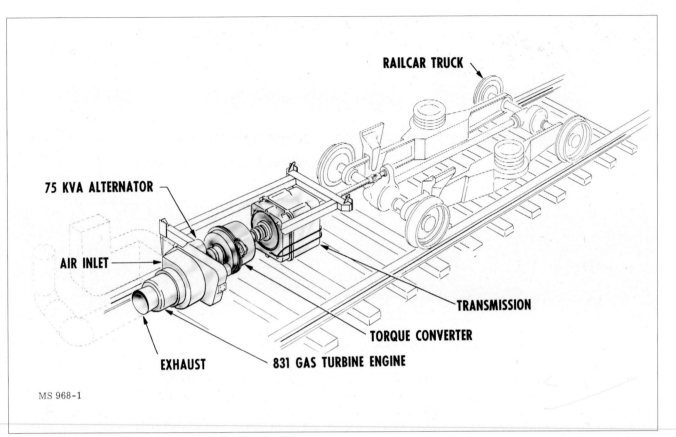

RAILCAR TRUCK

75 KVA ALTERNATOR

AIR INLET

TRANSMISSION

TORQUE CONVERTER

EXHAUST

831 GAS TURBINE ENGINE

MS 968-1

The GT-1 motive power system consisted of a small gas turbine, shown on left, which delivered power to an alternator (which provided electricity to the passenger car) and a mechanical transmission that delivered power to the axles. The GT-1 had two gas turbines, one for each truck. *Courtesy of Bill Mangahas*

A number of different experimental gas turbine cars and trains were tested on the Long Island Rail Road in the 1960s and '70s. These tests were intended to inform the Metropolitan Transportation Authority (owner of the LIRR) whether gas turbine technology could provide cost-effective, high-speed commuter rail service on the railroad's medium-to-low-use, non-electrified routes. If it could, then the MTA might avoid the costs associated with electrifying those lines.[158]

These federal- and state-funded MTA experiments proved the technical viability of turbine-powered commuter cars, but were not successful enough to convince the MTA to rely on this technology. They didn't produce a revolution in commuter rail car motive power. Diesel and electric motive power prevailed.

The first of these experiments was the GT-1 gas turbine commuter rail

car. It was unveiled to the public with the help of New York Governor Nelson Rockefeller on September 12, 1966, at the Ronkonkoma, N.Y., commuter rail station.[159]

The GT-1 was built by Budd Company and AiResearch Division of the Garrett Corporation by modifying an existing Budd passenger car. In the GT-1, two small gas turbines delivered power to torque converter transmissions, which in turn conveyed that power to the car's trucks via short drive shafts. One of the gas turbines also powered an alternator that produced electricity for heating, cooling, lighting, and control purposes.

While the GT-1 project was limited, an MTA report[160] stated it demonstrated that a gas turbine-powered commuter railcar could:

- Meet requirements for acceleration and top speed
- Cope with frequent start/stop cycles associated with commuter service

- Minimize vibration, noise, and emissions to acceptable levels
- Operate with "tolerable" fuel consumption based on mid-1960s fuel prices

In 1969, after successful tests, the same companies rebuilt the GT-1 into the GT-2, which used its gas turbines to power larger traction alternators that generated electricity to power four 150 horsepower electric traction motors mounted conventionally in the trucks. These electric traction motors enabled the GT-2 to also run off of electricity supplied by the LIRR's third-rail power system. Accordingly, it was a dual-mode railcar capable of operating on both electrified and non-electrified segments of its route.

This capability eliminated the need for car transfers at locations such as Jamaica station where the electrified system ended. The first run of the GT-2 on LIRR trackage was on March 23, 1970.[161] The GT-2 apparently ran

Long Island Rail Road No. 4003, a Garrett GT/E car, is at Oyster Bay, N.Y., July 2, 1977. Gas turbines were at a disadvantage with the long idle times typical of commuter equipment. *George E. Votava, Mike Boland collection*

for about a year before being retired.[162]

In 1975, the gas turbine commuter car experiment was taken a step further when the MTA introduced two, four-car gas turbine electric (GT/E) commuter trains, one built by General Electric and the other by Garrett.

These trains used Budd Company M1 passenger car bodies and were designed to achieve 90+ mph top speeds using 500-550 horsepower gas turbine engines in each car.[163] Like the GT-2, these were dual-mode and could operate either in an all-electric mode off a third-rail or in a gas turbine electric mode where the cars' gas turbines turned alternators that generated electricity for the traction motors.

The GT/E cars were not energy efficient. While they could take advantage of regenerative braking when operating on electrified third-rail, this energy conservation technology was not available to them once they were operating on turbine power. Predictably, the GT/E cars also demonstrated high fuel consumption when idling at station stops, where these cars consumed nearly 75% as much diesel fuel as they did when operating at 62-63% maximum output.[164]

Within a couple of years these gas turbine experiments were over. A summary report prepared for the MTA concluded that the gas turbine option was not attractive because the operating costs of gas turbine trains (energy, plus maintenance, plus refueling facilities costs) were expected to be high enough that it would be less expensive to electrify the lines instead.[165] In any event, when government funding dried up, the MTA lost interest in pursuing this alternative technology any further.

Figure 1.5-3 Interior of Garrett Turbine Module

The Garrett GT/E M-1 car turbine module was installed directly under the car's roofline but was actually external to the roof to prevent water leaks. To reduce turbine interior noise, the module was mounted using rubber isolating mounts. To further suppress noise, the module itself was encased in two layers of stainless steel separated by a layer of polyurethane foam. Turbine noise was described as "barely perceptible in a moving car." *Courtesy of Metropolitan Transportation Authority*

A General Electric GT/E M-1 car turbine compartment is shown with the exterior door open. The 550 horsepower ST6K gas turbines were industrial versions of Pratt and Whitney Aircraft of Canada Ltd. PT6 aircraft engines and were designed for quick-change replacement. The turbine, gear box, and generator were an integral assembly installed on rubber vibration isolation mounts. *Courtesy of Metropolitan Transportation Authority*

A United Aircraft TurboTrain races east through Milford, Conn., as Penn Central Train 3002 between New York and Boston on June 21, 1969. Penn Central and Amtrak hoped these trains would increase excitement while offering faster trips outside of the electrified Northeast Corridor between Boston and Washington, D.C. *Tom Nelligan*

Torque converter gas turbine train[166]

- 1968-1976 (1982 in Canada)
- 2,700 horsepower including head-end power
- Diesel fuel-fired
- Seven articulated trainsets in total (U.S. and Canada) designed and built by United Aircraft Corporation and Pullman
- Operated by Penn Central/ Amtrak and Canadian National/VIA

S tarting in 1969 and running through 2003, at least three different types of gas turbine-powered passenger trains operated in the United States and Canada. All of these used diesel fuel-fired gas turbines connected to torque converters or gear boxes to save weight and space compared to a GTEL configuration.

The primary purpose of these turbine-powered passenger trains was to introduce high-speed passenger train service to non-electrified Amtrak and Canadian National/Via Rail routes. It was hoped that these turbo trainsets would require less maintenance, be easier on the tracks, and capture public imagination, increasing ridership.

It was also hoped that the TurboTrain and other high-speed turbine trains like it would save (non-electrified) inter-city passenger rail in the 250-to-500-mile market where trains could be competitive with automobiles and planes.[167]

The first type of turbine-powered passenger train was the UAC TurboTrain, developed by Surface Transportation Systems of the Sikorsky Aircraft Division of the United Aircraft Corporation (UAC). Federal funding was provided by the High-Speed Ground Transportation Research and Development Act of 1965, championed by Senator Claiborne Pell, a Democrat representing Rhode Island.

During the years 1969-1976, two trainsets were operated in the U.S. between Boston and New York City by Penn Central and then Amtrak. At the

A TurboTrain speeds through the Pine Orchard section of Branford, Conn., on July 4, 1969. This was the original three-car configuration of these trains, which would later be lengthened to increase capacity. *Tom Nelligan*

A VIA Rail Turbo rests at the fueling rack at Spadina Yard, Toronto, Ontario, in September 1979. The trains would operate in Canada until 1982. *Roger Puta*

time, the Northeast Corridor was not electrified north of New Haven, Conn. An additional five trainsets ran in Canada between Toronto and Montreal from 1969 to 1982.

The new TurboTrain was characterized by UAC as being "stronger, lighter, faster, quieter, smoother, and cheaper" to operate than other passenger trains.[168] While it was possible to dismiss some of these claims as public relations hype, the UAC TurboTrains were technologically different, and their design definitely took aim at those goals.

Similar to an aircraft, UAC TurboTrain design stressed reduction of aerodynamic and mechanical drag accompanied by gas turbine power.[169] Its interior was described as roomy and modernistic, beyond what was then offered on airliners.[170] Initially known for a noisy and rough ride (including jerking movements rounding curves) when operating on less-than-perfect track, some improvements were made and noise issues were at least partially addressed by extensive sound-proofing after 1971.[171]

While the number of turbine engines and their horsepower could

vary, and different length trainsets were used, the 150-passenger, three-car Amtrak UAC TurboTrain configuration was reported to have six 400 horsepower ST6 UAC gas turbine engines, three per locomotive or power car at each end of a bi-directional articulated trainset.

Of the six turbines, five supplied power for traction purposes through reduction gears and what was called an "aerodynamic torque converter" associated with the turbine's "free turbine" design.[172] The other turbine (reported to be de-rated to 300 horsepower) rotated a generator to produce electricity for the locomotive's auxiliary functions and passenger cars' head-end power (HEP) requirements, such as lighting, heating, cooling, and ventilation.[173]

Making good on the gas turbine's promise to provide power at reduced weight per horsepower, these 400 horsepower turbine engines weighed just 300 pounds each and reportedly could be changed out in two hours or less.[174] The decision to use a mechanical transmission (i.e. gear box) instead of an electric transmission (i.e. alternator and electric traction motors) also saved

A Canadian National promotional brochure for its TurboTrain. Travel aboard the Turbo is depicted as glamorous and exciting. *Canadian National Railways*

TurboTrain™ Power Dome Car Interior
Rendering, Courtesy Canadian National Railways

Turbotrain's airplane-like luxury and glamor of the era were designed to challenge air travel for mid-length, 100-to-250 miles trips. Ironically, today's airliners hardly provide spaciousness and comfort. *Canadian National*

Large doors provided access to the TurboTrain's turbine engines. Maintenance is being performed at United Aircraft's Fields Point facility in Providence, R.I., on Oct. 13, 1969. *William D. Middleton*

weight, including unsprung weight that would have been rough on the rails.[175]

Amtrak eventually ran five-car TurboTrains and Canadian National ran two connected seven-car trainsets capable of carrying 600 passengers.[176] Canadian trainsets eventually used four 600 horsepower turbine engines for traction purposes and a 300 horsepower turbine for HEP.[177]

A number of design features enabled UAC's turbine trains to negotiate curves at 30% to 40% higher speeds than conventional passenger trains while producing less track damage.[178] These features included:

- A car-tilting system that supported cars above their centers of gravity by arms connected to the wheel bearings
- Low-riding cars that were 2.5 feet lower than conventional passenger cars and thus had a significantly lower center of gravity
- Single-axle trucks that were designed to guide wheels around curves
- Welded aluminum skin and frame construction by Pullman Standard created an exceptionally lightweight train that weighed half as much per passenger as conventional U.S. passenger trains[179]

The UAC TurboTrain's car-tilting technology was based on patents and designs purchased from the Chesapeake & Ohio Ry.'s so-called "Train X" project.[180] Train X contributed to the UAC TurboTrain articulation, lightweight aluminum construction, low center of gravity, and guided axles.[181]

Alan R. Cripe, who was C&O's

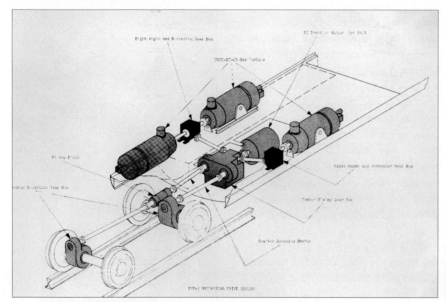

The power truck, right, and a schematic view of the gas turbines, generator, and gearboxes of the power dome car, above. Power for the train comes from two 400 horsepower ST6 gas turbines for propulsion and one for auxiliaries. The latter turbine is farthest to the right and is connected to an alternator that generated electricity for heating, cooling, lighting, and other services. Note that the traction motor is not located in the truck, but is connected to it and the axles via a driveshaft with gearbox. *William D. Middleton (right)/United Aircraft Corporation*

director of design, was responsible for many of these design innovations.[182] In fact, the April 1959 issue of *Trains* magazine contained a concept illustration of Cripe's for an advanced passenger train that looks like the UAC TurboTrain. Cripe's earlier concept would have been powered by two 300 horsepower diesel engines.[183] Cripe took his expertise to UAC and played a critical role designing the TurboTrain.[184]

The TurboTrain moved through the air with minimal aerodynamic drag, an important attribute once speeds exceeded 80 mph. Wind tunnel testing, consistent with the aircraft manufacturing origins of the TurboTrain, assisted in the design of an exceptionally smooth train. The windows were flush with the exterior and the diaphragms between cars were full width.

Like today's racing cars, even the bottoms of these train cars were aerodynamically addressed.[185] The lightweight aerodynamic design of the TurboTrain undoubtedly improved the trainset's energy efficiency in relative terms but didn't alter the gas turbine's inherent inefficiency at lower speeds or varying loads.

While not as fast as the fastest European passenger trains of that time, on December 20, 1967, a modified UAC TurboTrain reached a record speed of 170.8 mph as it passed Princeton Junction, N.J., on the Northeast Corridor.[186] Modifications included pulling the HEP engine out of its engine bay (installing it temporarily on the floor of one of the power cars) and installing re-rated 550 horsepower turbine engines in all six engine bays.[187] The TurboTrain's record as fastest U.S. production passenger train still stands. Of course, the turbine-powered train operated at much slower speeds in normal service.

With the UAC TurboTrain's operation coinciding with the increasing environmental consciousness (the first Earth Day was 1970), Sikorsky claimed[188] these environmental benefits:

- An outstanding 97% reduction in horsepower to transport passengers

Called a "free turbine engine," the United Aircraft ST6 400 horsepower gas turbine had separate shafts for the air compressor and its turbine and the output turbine. Each engine weighed only 300 pounds, significantly reducing the weight of these trains. *United Aircraft Corporation*

TurboTrain powerdome cars and coaches are under construction at Pullman-Standard's plant in Chicago. To cut weight, these trains were made of aluminum alloys, up to 1 inch thick in places to produce required strength. *Pullman-Standard*

The weight-saving single-axle trucks were radially guided to follow the curve of the track and supported the car's tilting mechanism. *William D. Middleton*

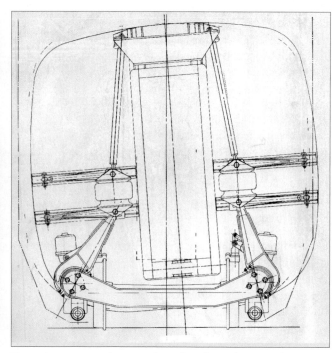

The unique suspension contributed to the TurboTrain's low center of gravity. The suspension supported the weight of each passenger car from arms mounted high above the single-axle trucks, enabling the cars to swing or bank pendulum-style when the trains negotiated curves. Higher speeds in curves were also enabled by a center of gravity nearly 2 feet lower than that of conventional passenger cars. *United Aircraft Corporation*

A United Aircraft TurboTrain in its first weeks of revenue service for Penn Central speeds through Cos Cob, Conn., on the former New York, New Haven & Hartford main line. It's freshly painted in its new PC colors on April 8, 1969. *Charles W. Stark*

compared to automobile use, e.g. a single TurboTrain with 2,000 horsepower could move 300 people between cities compared to 150 automobiles with 30,000 horsepower (assuming two people and 200 horsepower per car).

• A 75% reduction in air pollution per unit of horsepower
• Land preservation because the TurboTrain provided high speed rail capability without the need to construct new rights-of-way

United Aircraft computer modeling predicted that its TurboTrain should have been able to make the 437-mile trip from Buffalo, N.Y., to Grand Central Station in New York City in four hours and 49 minutes (respecting existing speed limits), compared to New York Central's seven hour, 53-minute schedule.[189]

However, despite its promise, the UAC TurboTrain didn't last long in U.S. service. While capable of genuinely high speeds, the TurboTrain was limited to 90 to 125 mph maximum speeds by track conditions. Maintenance costs were initially very high due to mechanical problems (axle gearboxes and suspension systems) and the need to operate a separate maintenance facility.

Eventually these turbine trains were reported to be operating with 96% availability.[190] However, fuel consumption was probably also an issue in a post-1973, Arab-Israel-War world with much higher oil prices.[191]

As its experiment with the UAC TurboTrains came to a close, Amtrak began another gas turbine trial, this time with proven French-built RTG Turboliners. These supplanted the UAC TurboTrains despite earlier optimism that many more TurboTrains would be running the rails.[192]

Whatever its faults, the UAC TurboTrain provided passengers with some treats. The power cars had high domes containing not only the engineer's cab but also 24 passenger seats. Passengers lucky enough to sit there could observe the engineer and his or her view forward. Shouldn't all passenger trains provide this experience?

One of the attractions of the power dome cars was the chance to watch the railroad ahead over the shoulder of the engineer, right, who's taking westbound Train 3001 from Boston to New York on Oct. 15, 1969. *William D. Middleton*

Out-of-service Amtrak UAC TurboTrains sit in storage at the coach yard behind 30th Street Station, in Philadelphia in 1981. TurboTrains last ran for Amtrak in 1976. *Mitch Goldman*

A Rohr-built Turboliner passes through Harmon, N.Y., in March 1982. The No. 163 power car ran as an RTL-I until 1996 when it was removed from service and upgraded to an RTL-III but never returned to service. The RTL Turboliners operating on the Buffalo-Albany-NYC route had dual-power capability. Visible on the right side of the track is the electric third rail. *Don Oltmann*

EXAMPLE 7: Amtrak RTG and RTL Turboliners

Torque converter gas turbine trains[193]
- 1973-2004
- 2,280-3,200 horsepower
- Diesel fuel-fired
- Six RTG trainsets by ANF Industrie; seven RTL trainsets by Rohr Industries/ANF Industrie
- Various models: RTG I, RTG II, RTL I, RTL II, RTL III
- Operated in U.S. by Amtrak

French ANF Industrie-built RTG Turboliner passenger trains that had proven themselves in France were purchased by Amtrak and operated on its Midwestern routes from 1973 to 1981. The acronym RTG stood for "Rame à Turbine à Gaz" or "Gas Turbine Train."[194] While fuel economy would become an issue, the benefits outlined in the chart, **1**, were attributed to the Turboliner[195] compared to diesel-electric locomotive-powered trains of the same capacity.

RTG trainsets were powered by two power cars, one in the front and one in the back of each trainset, each with a 1,140 horsepower Turbomecca Turmo III turboshaft gas turbine engine.

These were aeroderivative gas turbines, essentially helicopter engines modified to run on diesel fuel. The train's two turbine engines operated in unison as a result of command wires that ran the length of the train, connecting both engines to the lead power car's operating controls.[196] An additional Astazou turbine met HEP loads and was used to excite the traction generators.

Each turbine provided power through reduction gearing to a Voith hydraulic (also called hydrodynamic) transmission equipped with a torque-converter. This transmission was like a giant two-speed automobile automatic transmission.

With 1:1 and 2:1 gearing, it shifted gears at 79 mph, though the shifting was reported to be nearly unnoticed by passengers.[197] The output of this transmission was coupled to bogie (truck) axles by a cardan shaft.[198] This type of drive shaft contains U-joints to allow power transfer between unaligned rotating shafts.

In addition, each power car had an auxiliary power unit, or APU, consisting of a 430 horsepower gas turbine which rotated an alternator producing 300kw of electrical power. This electricity served the train's "hotel load," lighting, heating, air conditioning, and other non-tractive electric loads for passenger and power cars. Only one APU was needed and used at a time.[199]

The RTG Turboliner could initially

1 · Turboliner vs. diesel-hauled train

	Turbine Train	Diesel Train
Weight	293 tons	400 tons
Dynamic track force at 80 mph	70,000 pounds	110,000 pounds
Man-hours to replace engine	240 hours	850 hours
Availability	98%	92%
Maximum running speed on 1 degree curve with 3 inches of superelevation	112 mph	96 mph

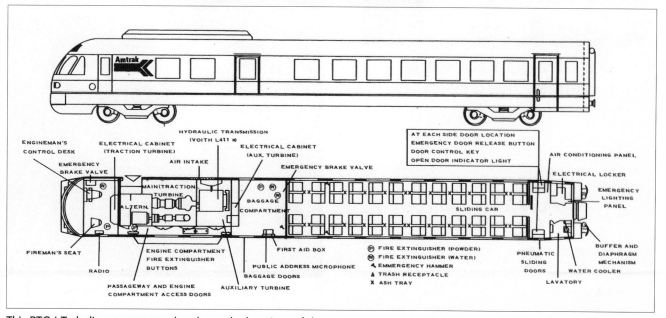

This RTG I Turboliner power car plan shows the locations of the major components. *ANF diagram, Dale A. Johnson collection*

Here come the Turboliners!

"Amtrak wanted to make a bold statement: to show that the company, and American rail passenger service, was about more than putting new decals on worn-out equipment. Amtrak wanted a train that would ignite public interest and imagination in a way that the Burlington Railroad's *Zephyr* had done 40 years earlier.

"In some ways, the Turboliners accomplished that goal. In scenes reminiscent of the *Zephyr*'s 1934 Denver-Chicago dash, the Turboliner's inaugural Chicago-St. Louis promotional trip drew thousands of spectators trackside—to station platforms, railroad crossings, backyards, and store and factory back doors—each pair of eyes hoping to catch a glimpse of the flashy red, white, and blue machine that brought together the jet engine and the flanged wheel."

—*Dale A. Johnson*
author, Trail of the Turbo: The Amtrak Turboliner Story

Turboliner roster

RTG power cars			
Delivered	Number	Rebuild	Retired
1973	60/61	-	1981
1973	62/63	-	1981
1975	58/59	-	1981
1975	64/65	1988	1994 (64), 1995 (65)
1975	66/67	1987	1994 (66), 1995 (67)
1975	68/69	1988	1995

RTL power cars			
Delivered	Number1	Rebuild	Retired
1976	150/151	RTL III, 2003 (150)	2004
1976	152/153	-	
1976	154/155	RTL III, 2003 (155)	2004
1976	156/157	-	
1976	158/159	RTL II, 1994 (159); RTL III, 2003 (158)	2004
1976	160/161	RTL III, 2003 (161)	2004
1977	162/163	RTL III, 2003 (162, 163)	2004

This is the gas turbine train Amtrak has chosen.

On February 28, 1973 Amtrak contracted with ANF-FRANGECO Paris for delivery of two of the latest Turbo-powered trainsets: the "RTG". They are destined for the Chicago-Milwaukee and Chicago-St. Louis runs.

ANF-FRANGECO built the ETG and RTG gas turbine trainsets for SNCF-French National Railways. ETG trains have already totalled over 5 million miles on the regular Paris-Caen and Paris-Cherbourg service during the past two years.

By courtesy of the SNCF two trains of the current completely air-conditioned five-car RTG production series will be released to Amtrak during Summer 1973.

ANF-FRANGECO

Tour Aurore / Cedex 5 / Courbevoie / 92 Paris La Defense / France
U.S. Representatives: Allied International Corporation
230 Park Avenue, New York, N.Y. .... Tel. 689-6126

An ANF advertisement from the Jan. 14, 1974, issue of *Railway Age* magazine touts its new customer, Amtrak. *Dale A. Johnson collection*

An Amtrak Turboliner navigates the maze of switches leaving Union Station in Chicago on March 22, 1978. *Tom Golden/Sam Beck Collection*

Train 350, an RTG I Turboliner, waits for passengers at the Ann Arbor, Mich., station on May 29, 1975. *Dale A. Johnson*

Amtrak's RTG Turboliner was featured on the 1975 timetable touting Midwest service. *Amtrak*

accelerate at just over 1 mph/second, but took 350 seconds to travel from 0 to 100 mph.[200] This is slow by automobile standards, but was acceptable for non-electric passenger trains. This acceleration rate was enabled by passenger cars that weighed 30% less than conventional cars while having the same seating capacity.[201]

However, braking from 100 mph took over three-quarters of a mile (4,400 feet) under normal conditions. The RTG was equipped with three different braking systems: Hydrodynamic braking (using the torque converter to retard speed), wheel tread brakes, and disc brakes.[202] Since this trainset was not a GTEL, dynamic braking (using electric motors as generators) was not an option.

The hydrodynamic brakes were unique. When in braking mode, a spinning rotor within the transmission—powered by the power car's rotating axles—would be exposed to stationary rotor blades in an oil-filled casing. The ensuing friction would produce a retarding force while quickly heating up the oil.

This hot oil was pumped from the casing and cooled by a large heat exchanger or radiator. The cooling load of this radiator was so high that the fan that blew ambient air over it was mechanically driven; the HEP

generator couldn't handle it.[203]

The RTG Turboliners were tested to 125 mph, although along all Midwestern routes they were limited to a maximum of 79 mph due to track conditions. An ANF Industrie brochure claimed that its gas turbine locomotive lent itself to high speed running because the low weight of the turbine engines allowed low axle loadings—16 to 18 tons per driven axle compared to 19 to 30 tons with diesel traction. Low axle loadings improve stability and minimize track damage.[204]

In 1973, Amtrak praised its RTG Turboliner fleet claiming it "offered the advantages of jet travel, yet it never leaves the ground,"[205] and, "you glide down the tracks so smoothly you can scarcely feel the rails."[206] Then, in 1976, Amtrak celebrated the arrival of its new RTL Turboliners with an advertising campaign themed, "The Train of the 21st Century Has Arrived Years Ahead of Schedule."

The RTL Turboliners—which could be expanded to six or seven cars—operated between New York City and Buffalo/Niagara Falls and between New York City and Montreal from 1976 to 2004. These were designed and constructed as a joint venture between French ANF Industrie (which was purchased by Bombardier

in 1989) and U.S. Rohr Industries.

ANF provided the car bodies, wheelsets, and engines, and Rohr provided the cabs, car interiors, and other U.S. components. Rohr assembled the trains in its Chula Vista, Calif., plant.[207] RTL stood for "Rohr Turbo Liner," though Turboliner was spelled as a single word.[208]

Like the RTG Turboliners, RTLs used gas turbine propulsion systems. However, consistent with New York City's environmental regulations, RTL power cars were also equipped with a 300 horsepower electric traction motor to provide motive power for the 33-mile trip between Croton-Harmon and New York City's Grand Central Terminal and Pennsylvania ("Penn") Station.

Third-rail pickup provided 600-volt DC electricity for these motors. When operating in electric-only mode, the RTL Turboliner's maximum speed was just 45 mph.[209]

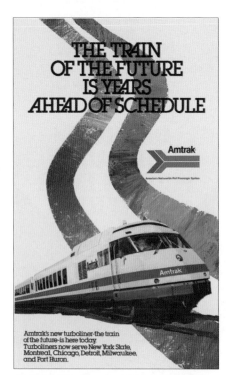

An RTL Turboliner brochure sports the message "The Train of the Future" has arrived! *Amtrak*

Track improvements funded by a New York State transportation bond initiative allowed the Rohr-built Turboliners to travel at 110 mph along various track sections west and south of Albany, N.Y.

Maintenance for the New York Turboliner fleet was carried out in Amtrak's Rensselaer, N.Y., locomotive shop. In order to address potential operational problems, Amtrak assigned a mechanical department employee to each Turboliner run, which added significant cost. Eventually, 18 technicians (informally called "train riders") were required to meet this need for 10 operational Turboliners, given layovers at end points and vacation and sick day coverage.[210]

In 1986, after successful testing in France, upgraded gas turbine engines were installed in half of the RTL power cars as well as in the RTG II trainsets, which were rebuilt from 1987 to 1988. These Turmo XII engines produced 1,542 horsepower. When a Turmo XII power car was paired with a 1,140 horsepower Turmo III power car, the resulting RTL Turboliner would have 2,682 horsepower and associated performance improvement. The new turbine engines were also more energy efficient.

The fuel efficiency of locomotive engines is measured in terms of brake specific fuel consumption (BSFC). Brake specific fuel consumption is the amount of fuel burned (in units of pounds of diesel fuel) to produce a given amount of work at the engine's crankshaft (in units of horsepower-hours). A lower BSFC means greater efficiency.

The BSFC of the Turmo III was 0.689 while the BSFC of the Turmo XII was 0.563. Thus, the Turmo XII provided an 18% improvement in efficiency.[211] Since BSFC here represents peak fuel economy when the engine is operating under optimal

1991 Amtrak Turboliner poster art depicts an RTL I Turboliner passing under New York City's George Washington Bridge on its way north to Albany, N.Y., and beyond. *Amtrak*

The June 12, 1978, *Railway Age* cover features a beautiful Don Ball Jr., photograph of a Turboliner speeding alongside the Hudson River on an Albany-to-NYC run. *Don Ball Jr./Railway Age*

near full-load conditions, it's only partly indicative of actual overall fuel economy.

As a point of reference, the EMD SD60 diesel-electric locomotive of that era used the EMD 710 engine which had a (peak) BSFC of 0.340 plus the diesel engine's advantage throughout the duty cycle when compared to gas turbines. Overall, the diesel engine probably would have been twice as efficient as the gas turbine.

As noted earlier, the duty cycle of railroad locomotives involves changing speeds and loads, including substantial idle time. This duty cycle adversely impacts the fuel economy of both gas turbine and diesel-electric locomotives, but hurts gas turbines more because their fuel economy drops off more quickly at part-load and lower speeds.

Amtrak was keenly aware of this and compensated by encouraging its engineers to run the Turboliners on only one gas turbine engine once the trainsets were up to speed. This made sense because it was more efficient to operate one engine close to fully loaded instead of two engines under a lighter load.[212] Testing in 1980 had shown that, depending on the ability and enthusiasm of the crew, it was possible to use this strategy while maintaining the schedule.

Amtrak was also aware that fuel could be conserved by altering schedules so that Turboliners could travel at higher speeds uninterrupted for longer periods of time. This could have been accomplished by reducing the number of stops or providing passenger trains greater priority on freight railroad trackage. While average speeds of 50 mph were the norm, the trainset's optimum speed for fuel economy was 80 mph.[213]

A less technical way of understanding the fuel economy differential of the Turboliners vs. diesel-electric motive power is to compare actual fuel consumption over a given route. On a round-trip between Albany, N.Y., and New York City, an RTL Turboliner routinely consumed 825 gallons of diesel fuel, while a GE Genesis diesel-electric passenger locomotive consumed 550 gallons.[214] Here, the Turboliner consumed 50% more fuel while hauling fewer cars and fewer passengers.[215]

The differential was greater than that if the full round trip was defined as including the Sunnyside Yard in Queens, N.Y., and the serving and inspection facility in Rensselaer, N.Y. At Sunnyside the HEP turbine would run for hours, and at Rensselaer the trainset would be moved around the yard at low speeds.

The Turboliner's turbine exhaust temperature of 1,290°F was also indicative of energy wastefulness. This was reduced to 600-700°F before being ejected from the locomotive's stack by diluting it with ambient air in the engine's silencer or muffler. RTG and RTL exhaust could damage overhead structures if the trains were parked underneath them.[216]

By the mid-1990s, after 20 years of service, RTL trainsets had traveled millions of miles and were in need of refurbishment.[217] Updated units became the RTL II and RTL III trainsets.

In August of 1995, the U.S. Federal Railroad Administration released a report describing Amtrak test results of the first RTL II Turboliner.[218] This model and the yet-to-come RTL III were equipped with new 1,600 horsepower digitally controlled Turmomecca TM-1600 Makila T1 engines.

These industrial turbines were more energy efficient and reliable.[219] The FRA

Life in the fast lane—Remembering the Turboliner

"When regular Turboliner through-service to New York City commenced in the fall of 1976, New York State was anxious to show off the taxpayer-funded track improvements and engineers were instructed to make announcements when the top speed of 110 had been reached. However, not all passengers were interested in knowing how fast they were going, and I well remember being on an eastbound trip when an elderly woman in our car experienced a 'panic attack' upon learning of our high speed. These public announcements were soon discontinued.

"Turboliner exhaust gas temperatures were extremely high and great care was taken to avoid stopping the power cars under bridges or structures which might catch on fire. While the turbines were supposed to be off when the Turboliners were operating in New York City tunnels and in Grand Central Station, at least once a Turboliner parked on a storage track under a portion of the station was fired up by mistake. The resulting heat from the jet exhaust buckled the thick concrete slab overhead and also the thinner overlaid marble floor in the public area above the power car.

"In later years, several fires did occur at Penn Station (after Amtrak had moved operations there from Grand Central in 1991), which led Amtrak to greatly curtail Turboliner use based on safety concerns."

—*Bruce B. Becker, Vice-President Operations, Rail Passenger Association*

The RTL Turboliner brochure promises "The Train of the Future" has arrived! *Amtrak*

The train of the 21st century has arrived years ahead of schedule.

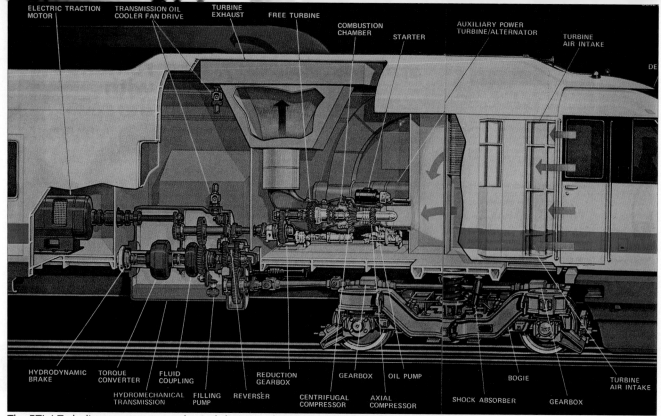

Labels on diagram (top): ELECTRIC TRACTION MOTOR · TRANSMISSION OIL COOLER FAN DRIVE · TURBINE EXHAUST · FREE TURBINE · COMBUSTION CHAMBER · STARTER · AUXILIARY POWER TURBINE/ALTERNATOR · TURBINE AIR INTAKE · DE

Labels on diagram (bottom): HYDRODYNAMIC BRAKE · TORQUE CONVERTER · FLUID COUPLING · HYDROMECHANICAL TRANSMISSION · FILLING PUMP · REVERSER · REDUCTION GEARBOX · CENTRIFUGAL COMPRESSOR · AXIAL COMPRESSOR · GEARBOX · OIL PUMP · SHOCK ABSORBER · BOGIE · GEARBOX · TURBINE AIR INTAKE

The RTL I Turboliner power car mechanical design is shown in a cutaway diagram. Shown here are the gas turbine, reduction gearing, torque converter, hydrodynamic brake, gear boxes, and the cardan drive shaft (in green, between the reverser and the gearbox mounted on the truck, which, oddly enough, isn't labeled). *Rohr Industries diagram, Dale A. Johnson collection*

report stated that the RTL II consumed only 580 gallons for the round-trip between Albany, N.Y., and New York City.[220] This was a 30% improvement over the RTL.

The FRA report also documented much faster acceleration by the RTL II, but noted that the RTL II still took twice as much time to reach 125 mph as the AEM-7 electric locomotives pulling passenger trains on the Northeast Corridor.

RTL II braking from 125 mph took approximately 6,500 feet—well over one mile—but easily consistent with Amtrak requirements.[221] The FRA hoped that Turboliner braking would eventually be enhanced by regenerative braking utilizing flywheels, but this improvement never came to pass. Comically, Amtrak tested RTL II wheel-slip by pouring a 50-foot long, ¼-inch wide bead of dishwashing detergent on both rails ahead of the RTL II power car.[222]

An RTL III trainset reached 144 mph between Albany and Hudson, N.Y., during February 15-16, 2001, test runs.[223]

The RTG and RTL Turboliners provided Amtrak effective service for 30 years and on that basis alone must

An RTL I Turboliner heads eastbound through Jordan, N.Y. with an *Empire Service* train in the mid-to-early 1990s. Turboliners ran out of New York until 2004. *Matt Donnelly*

be judged successful. These unique trains rode the rails smoothly, attracted attention and ridership when first introduced, and for many years achieved availability of 90% or more.

While Amtrak didn't issue a press release explaining why it ceased running Turboliners, the list of reasons undoubtedly included inferior fuel economy compared to diesel-electric motive power and a growing collection of large and small maintenance

problems. These problems ranged from inadequate air conditioning to the high cost of turbine overhaul and replacement, e.g. $200,000 and $830,000, respectively, for the Makila engine.[224]

EXAMPLE 8: Compressed Integrated Natural Gas Locomotive (CINGL)

Initial planning for an 8,000 horsepower compressed natural gas-fired gas turbine electric locomotive for Canadian and U.S. operation began in 1994. The unique project was spearheaded by Applied Power & Propulsion, a Vancouver, B.C.-based railroad systems company that later was reorganized into Railpower, manufacturer of Green Goat hybrid switcher and genset locomotives.[226]

The proposed locomotive was called CINGL for "Compressed Integrated Natural Gas Locomotive." Potentially configured as an A- or B-unit (a locomotive without an operator's cab), the CINGL would have been a GTEL with the gas turbine rotating a direct-drive high-speed alternator to produce AC electricity to power inverters and AC traction motors.

Applied Power's partners were Allison/Rolls-Royce, Allied Signal, and EDO Energy Company. Interest in a natural gas locomotive of this type was prompted by historically low natural gas prices (compared to diesel fuel prices) and the potential design advantages of pairing this fuel with a gas turbine.

The 8,000 horsepower CINGL would have replaced two 3,600 horsepower SD60s, but it would have cost more than twice as much as these diesel-electric locomotives: $3.7 million for one CINGL compared to $2.66 million for two SD60s at the time.[227] This drawback would have been more

than offset by the CINGL's fuel cost savings potential. Unfortunately, the rising price of natural gas effectively canceled this project just three years later without a single prototype being built.[228]

Prior to 1994, railroad experimentation with liquefied natural gas (LNG) fuel in diesel-electric

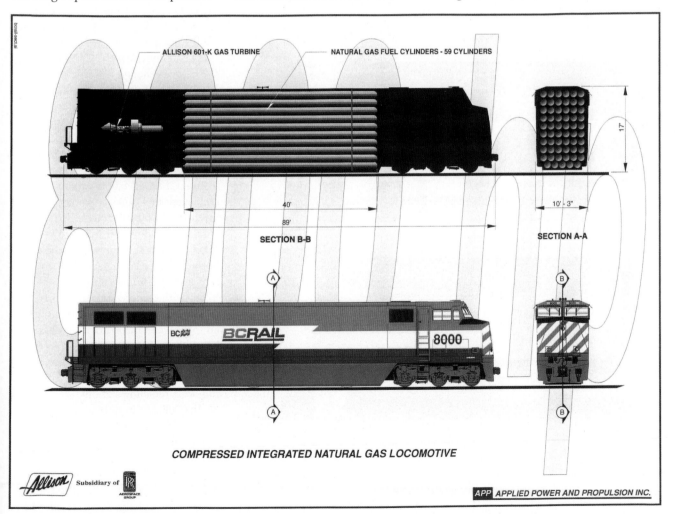

ALLISON 601-K GAS TURBINE   NATURAL GAS FUEL CYLINDERS - 59 CYLINDERS

17'

40'

89'

10' - 3'

SECTION B-B

SECTION A-A

BCRAIL   8000

COMPRESSED INTEGRATED NATURAL GAS LOCOMOTIVE

Allison Subsidiary of Rolls-Royce AEROSPACE GROUP

APP APPLIED POWER AND PROPULSION INC.

This concept design illustration shows a proposed Compressed Integrated Natural Gas Locomotive (CINGL). It would carry 59 cylinders of compressed natural gas and an Allison gas turbine and generator. *Applied Power & Propulsion* locomotives had been a mixed bag, which did not lead to significant use of this fuel for rail propulsion. Diesel locomotives could be converted to run effectively on a natural gas/diesel fuel blend,[229] but potential fuel cost savings had to be balanced against high costs for locomotive engine modifications, addition of a tender, and a new, parallel fueling infrastructure. As a result, railroads might achieve a modest return on investment with natural gas fueling while exposing themselves to substantial risk if natural gas prices rose faster than diesel fuel prices. Applied Power and its partners believed the CINGL gas turbine with compressed

natural gas (CNG) could substantially reduce costs and therefore risks.

As previously explained, a gas turbine can provide a lot of horsepower in a small, lightweight package. The power density of the gas turbine was a key design consideration for the CINGL, which would have used an Allison advanced 571-K gas turbine capable of producing 9,000 shaft horsepower.[230] While CINGL would have been 89 feet long and weighed 390,000 pounds, the 571-K engine was less than 7 feet long and weighed just 2,000 pounds.[231]

Unlike a diesel engine, it did not require a cooling system. That left

plenty of capacity for the CINGL to carry its other propulsion equipment (alternator, inverters, etc.) and, in its cab-equipped configuration, 59 40-foot long cylinders of compressed natural gas containing an amount of energy equal to 8,000 gallons of diesel fuel. These specially designed cylinders would have weighed one-third as much as conventional steel cylinders and one-half as much as composite-wrapped aluminum cylinders.[232]

Even in compressed or liquefied form, natural gas fuel has a much lower energy density than diesel fuel. Compressed natural gas, or CNG, needs approximately four times the space to provide the same amount of energy as diesel fuel. Liquefied natural gas or LNG is denser than CNG, but it still requires approximately two times the space to provide the same amount of energy as diesel fuel.[233] In addition, being a cryogenic liquid, LNG requires specially insulated tanks to maintain its -260°F temperature.

The designers of the CINGL chose CNG, even though it was less dense, because it was significantly cheaper to produce and store on and off the locomotive. They also had room for an abundance of it within the locomotive thanks to their selection of a compact gas turbine prime mover.

The CINGL's 8,000-gallon equivalent fuel capacity would have given it a 1,000-mile range. That would have allowed it to be slow-filled (with gas compressors only) at both ends of a Vancouver, B.C., to Chicago or Toronto run while quick-filled (with compressors and buffered pressurized storage) two or three times en route when mandatory 1,000-mile inspections were conducted. Thus, overall natural gas costs would have been reduced by requiring only three full-scale refueling stations.

The Allison gas turbine was energy efficient for an engine of its type, but it was still less energy efficient than locomotive diesel engines of that era. While the turbine had a peak efficiency of 33% at full power,[234] the diesel engine in an SD60 had a peak energy efficiency of approximately 40.8%, based on the aforementioned BSFC of 0.340.[235]

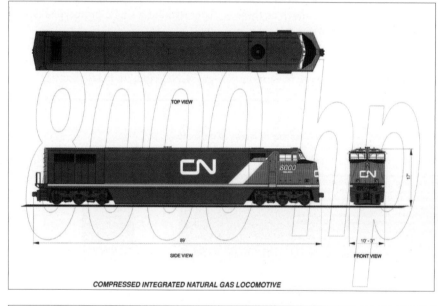

COMPRESSED INTEGRATED NATURAL GAS LOCOMOTIVE

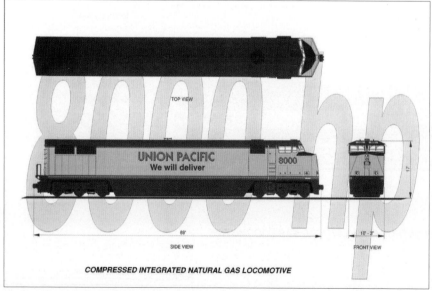

COMPRESSED INTEGRATED NATURAL GAS LOCOMOTIVE

Other candidates for the proposed CINGL were Canadian National and Union Pacific.
Applied Power & Propulsion

Even more importantly, the turbine's efficiency dropped off much more rapidly in lower throttle settings than did the diesel engine. At the equivalent of Notch 1, 2, and 3 throttle settings on a diesel, the turbine's efficiency was just 7%, 12%, and 18%, respectively.[236] When idling, the gas turbine would have been even more wasteful than the diesel engine.

The CINGL's theoretical full-load peak fuel-to-rail efficiency can be calculated as follows:

Assumptions
0.33 gas turbine full-load efficiency
0.95 alternator efficiency
0.96 inverter efficiency
0.96 traction motor efficiency
0.99 gears and wheels efficiency

0.33 x 0.95 x 0.96 x 0.95 x 0.99
= 0.286 or 28.9% peak
fuel-to-rail efficiency

CINGL's fuel-to-rail energy efficiency would have dropped to 6% at a Notch 1 power output, 10% in Notch 2, and 15% in Notch 3.

To overcome a gas turbine locomotive's propensity for very poor fuel economy when at low load and idling, Applied Power President Frank Donnelly proposed an operating strategy that would maximize the time the CINGL operated at near or full load and minimize the time the locomotive operated in low power settings or idling.[237] This duty cycle was better suited to a gas turbine's efficiency curve and could be accomplished by:
• Operating the CINGL only on uncongested routes where it could spend as much time as possible at full power
• Pairing the CINGL with a conventional diesel-electric locomotive so that the CINGL didn't have to be operated continuously when pulling a train
• Turning off the CINGL when in yards
• Operating it as much as possible in on/off mode where "on" was at or near full power
Applied Power believed this energy

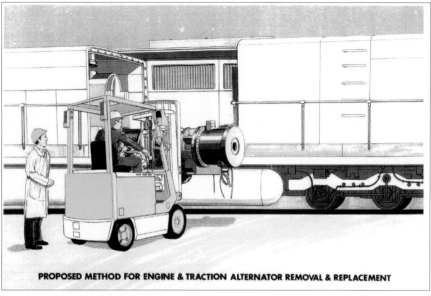

PROPOSED METHOD FOR ENGINE & TRACTION ALTERNATOR REMOVAL & REPLACEMENT

The compact size of the turbine power plant makes engine replacement a relatively simple task. *Applied Power & Propulsion*

conservation strategy could best be implemented on Canadian National's relatively flat route between Winnipeg and Vancouver. Six test locomotives were envisioned for this railroad. BC Rail, Burlington Northern, and Union Pacific were other potential early customers.

Beyond energy conservation, the CINGL concept had additional advantages or selling points. The CINGL's ability to deliver 8,000 horsepower to the rails through two three-axle trucks would have caused less track damage than delivering that much horsepower through four three-axle trucks on two SD60s. Track repair savings were estimated to be $500,000 to $1,000,000 over a 10- to 15-year period.[238]

Six 1,600 horsepower electric traction motors that were available at the time were envisioned for the CINGL. That's a lot of horsepower per axle but the CINGL's use of AC traction would have provided improved traction control and adhesion. The CINGL would also have been much quieter than Union Pacific's GTELs.[239]

In the lead-up to Applied Power's critical IEEE/ASME Joint Rail Conference paper, Donnelly described the "big 8,000 hp CINGL" as providing "economies of scale where fewer units really hit a home run for operating ratios." The CINGL

would provide "twice the horsepower for roughly half the fuel cost" while reducing nitrogen oxide emissions by 85%.[240]

Immediately after the IEEE/ASME conference, a Vancouver, B.C., newspaper[241] declared "Gas Turbine is on Track," noting that BC Rail computer modeling revealed that the railroad could achieve a 37% fuel cost savings with the CINGL compared to diesel-electric locomotive operation. Donnelly commented, "The study results are staggering. There has never been a scenario like this since dieselization." Unfortunately, the promise of CINGL was never realized.

The reliability, efficiency and the interoperability of modern diesel-electric locomotives (their ability to roam continent-wide) would have made the introduction of the CINGL very difficult for general uses in the North American pool. However, in "captive service," CINGL deployment might have been possible under certain economic conditions.

EXAMPLE 9: **BOMBARDIER JETTRAIN**

Gas turbine electric locomotive (GTEL)[242]
- 2000-2002
- 5,000-8,000 horsepower
- Diesel fuel-fired
- Prototype designed and built by Bombardier Transportation
- Intended for Amtrak

The Bombardier JetTrain was proposed to bring high-speed rail to non-electrified routes. It was put through its paces at the Transportation Technology Center in Pueblo, Colo. During testing, the locomotive with three passenger cars reached 156 mph. *Bombardier Transportation*

In 1997, the Federal Railroad Administration solicited proposals to develop high-speed locomotives and trainsets for Amtrak's non-electrified Northeast Corridor routes.[243] Specifically, the objective was to develop a locomotive/trainset capable of matching the rapid acceleration and 150 mph top speed of Amtrak's high-speed electric Acela trainsets without incurring the cost of the electric catenary infrastructure ($3.5 million per mile[244]) used to power electric locomotives and trains.

Bombardier was selected and began work on the project in 1998, designing and building a gas turbine locomotive prototype. It was nicknamed the "Acela Express" because it looked like a power car for the Bombardier/Alstom-built Amtrak Acela. The $25 million estimated cost of developing the locomotive was to be split between Bombardier and the Federal Railroad Administration.[245]

Like the Acela and the UAC TurboTrain many years before it, the Bombardier JetTrain would have carriage-tilting technology to allow for faster speeds around curves. The prototype was tested successfully at routine speeds of 130 mph while pulling conventional Amtrak passenger cars. Significantly, the Bombardier JetTrain demonstrated a top speed of 156 mph.[156] This was more than 30 mph faster than the Siemens and Progress Rail/EMD diesel-electric passenger locomotives Amtrak and U.S.

This image is from a Bombardier brochure titled "Travelling at the Speed of Nonstop." It begins, "There is something about trains. We love them, ride them and wave at them. For decades Europeans have combined their love of trains with the advantages of high-speed rail. Bombardier JetTrain technology builds upon our European experience to bring high-speed rail to America. It's America's turn!" *Bombardier Transportation*

Its appearance modeled after the Amtrak Acela, Bombardier's JetTrain prototype gas turbine locomotive was on display at VIA Rail's Montreal Maintenance Center on Sept. 6, 2003. *Michel Robichaud*

regional passenger train operators are now phasing in.

The prime mover in this gas turbine locomotive was a diesel fuel-fired Pratt & Whitney PW 150 turboprop jet engine that produced 5,000 shaft horsepower.[247] This was used to generate electricity for the locomotive's AC traction motors, which had a continuous rating of 4,400 horsepower.[248]

The lightweight nature of the turbine—said to weigh just 5% of a diesel engine of comparable horsepower output (882 pounds vs. 22,046 pounds[249])—reduced the weight of the locomotive by a remarkable 20%.[250] Bombardier noted that its lightweight, high-powered prototype had "the highest power-to-weight ratio for a fuel-powered locomotive in North America."[251] This design feature, along with its reduced unsprung weight,

enabled the locomotive to operate at higher speeds with less track damage.

Bombardier claimed its JetTrain locomotive would achieve at least a 30% reduction in greenhouse gas emissions compared to an equivalent diesel-electric locomotive, presumably because of the locomotive's lighter weight plus other improvements that contributed to better fuel economy.[252]

For example, to overcome the inefficiency of gas turbines at lower speeds and lighter loads, this Bombardier locomotive was designed to use its head-end power[253] diesel engine for starting the locomotive and running it at speeds below 30 mph.[254]

The electric generator in this prototype locomotive was a French TGV traction motor. AC electric traction motors function as electrical generators when torque is applied to

their shafts while their field windings are energized.

One report stated that a flywheel was planned to enable the locomotive to have regenerative braking capability wherein the mechanical energy recovered from braking would be stored in a spinning flywheel and available for later locomotive propulsion.[255] Discharging the flywheel could have released as much as 3,000 additional horsepower.

The alternative to regenerative braking is dynamic braking, with the electricity generated by the traction motors in braking mode being converted to heat in roof-top dynamic braking grids that dissipate the heat to the atmosphere. Bombardier could have also used the strategy being employed by Siemens and Progress Rail/ EMD's new diesel-electric passenger

The project was jointly funded by the Federal Railroad Administration and Bombardier. *Michel Robichaud*

The JetTrain was tested with Amtrak cars and successfully reached 130 mph as a matter of routine. *Michel Robichaud*

locomotives, namely, to use recovered braking energy to partially power auxiliary and HEP loads.

The JetTrain project began with high hopes, with the president and CEO of Bombardier Transportation, Pierre Lortie, stating that his company had "moved the goalposts" and that "JetTrain high-speed rail is game-changing technology that breaks open

the high-speed market throughout North America."

But this didn't happen. The JetTrain failed to receive further funding. Proposals to use the JetTrain in Canada and the United Kingdom also never caught on. Thus, this potentially impressive high-speed GTEL locomotive was never developed beyond a single locomotive prototype.

The fastest turbine-powered locomotive and train[256]

The Turboliners, TurboTrain, and JetTrain were all fast, or at least looked fast, but the real speed demon among gas turbine locomotives was the French TGV[257] Alstom-built gas turbine prototype train No. 001. This train—consisting of three coaches permanently coupled to power cars on each end—achieved 198 mph in a test run way back in December 8, 1972.[258]

While No. 001 was preceded by at least one other French gas turbine locomotive, No. 001 was one-of-a-kind. After experimenting with this extraordinary prototype, the French national railroad (SNCF) decided to power its high-speed rail fleet with electric locomotives running off catenary. But that endeavor was influenced by what was learned operating the No. 001. Key areas of research with the No. 001 were aerodynamics, braking, and high-speed stability. To enhance stability, the No. 001 had a "hunting control" system that prevented the trainset from oscillating or bouncing back and forth between the rails. Unsprung weight was also reduced by installing the electric traction motors in the vehicle body instead of on the truck or bogie.

The high-speed gas turbine TGV 001 was featured on the cover of the April 1972 issue of the French railfan magazine *La Vie du Rail*. *F. Fénino, Photorail-SNCF*

The TGV prototype awaits passengers at Austerlitz Station in Paris in the summer of 1973. In 1972, the train—three coaches and two power cars—reached 198 mph during testing. *Jean-Marc Frybourg*

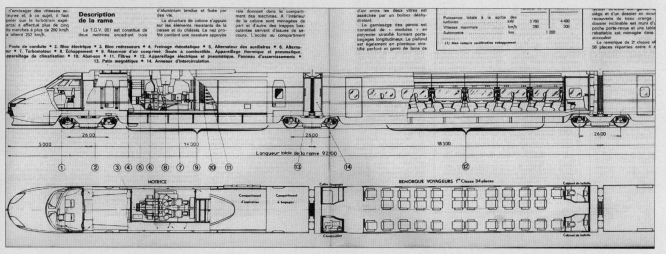

Side and top cutaway views of TGV 001 printed in the April 1972 issue of *La Vie du Rail* show the location of the components. *La Vie du Rail*

Each of No. 001's power cars had two gas turbine engines providing a total of 4,800 to 6,400 horsepower, depending on which Turmo gas turbines were used.[259] The turboshaft gas turbines rotated an alternator to generate electricity for electric traction motors on each of the train's 12 axles. Being a GTEL, the train was also equipped with dynamic braking (referred to as rheostatic braking by the French) as well as three other braking systems.[260]

Remarkably, over the course of 34,000 miles of testing over 200 km/hr (125 mph),[261] the No. 001 is credited with 175 runs in excess of 300 km/hr (186 mph).[262] The No. 001 still holds the record as the world's fastest non-electric train. It was retired in 1978 after the case for turbine tractive power for high-speed rail was undermined by fuel economy and fuel cost issues, and by the proven success of all-electric high-speed operation under catenary.[263]

4

An atomic steam turbine locomotive – what could possibly go wrong?!

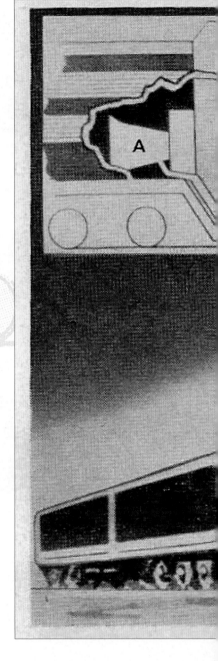

In the early 1950s, University of Utah physics professor Dr. Lyle Borst (1912-2002) and his graduate students in a nuclear technology course developed and proposed an atomic steam turbine electric locomotive.[264] Borst had worked on the Manhattan Project, which produced the first atomic bombs a decade earlier. His atomic locomotive never came to fruition, but it nonetheless represented an unusual and interesting part of the turbine locomotive story and is worth telling here.

Atoms for war and peace

Let's begin by briefly examining the historical context of the atomic locomotive. In 1945, the United States dropped atomic bombs on Hiroshima and Nagasaki. These bombs incinerated the two cities with an explosive power equal to 15,000 to 20,000 tons of TNT each. While the use of atomic weapons ended World War II, they also began an arms race and Cold War between the United States and Soviet Union.

In 1949, the Soviet Union exploded its first atomic bomb. This was followed in 1952 by the U.S. test explosion of a 10-megaton hydrogen, or thermonuclear, bomb that was 500 times more powerful than the atomic

An art Deco illustration of Lyle Borst's atomic train shows the leading cab unit which would have carried a 9-cubic-foot nuclear reactor contained within a massive radiation shield evident on the side of the locomotive. The second unit in this 160-foot-long atomic STEL would have carried radiators and fans for cooling and water recovery. The inset shows a stylistic cutaway of the nuclear reactor. *April 1954, Popular Mechanics*

bombs preceding it. In 1953, the Soviet Union detonated its first hydrogen bomb. That similar nuclear weapons capability could be developed by other countries was demonstrated when the United Kingdom tested its first atomic bomb in 1952.

Atomic bombs derive their energy from splitting uranium and plutonium atoms in a process called atomic fission. In contrast, hydrogen bombs release

energy through atomic fusion, binding hydrogen atoms together to form helium atoms. The high temperatures required for fusion are created in a hydrogen bomb by an atomic bomb at its core.

These early developments alarmed many Americans, especially atomic scientists who feared that their invention had set the world on a course where humanity itself might perish.

Meanwhile, the governments of both the United States and the Soviet Union promoted nuclear fission for non-military purposes.

This idea was formally expressed by President Dwight D. Eisenhower when he gave his famous "Atoms for Peace" speech to the United Nations on December 8, 1953.[265] Eisenhower sounded the alarm about the dangers of atomic war and the nuclear arms

Will atomic energy power tomorrow's railroads?

Some day you may see a train like this — powered by the energy locked up in the atom.

Possibly the locomotive will have its own nuclear reactor. Or perhaps it will use electricity generated at atomic power stations. But this much is certain. Of all forms of land transportation, railroads offer the greatest opportunities for the efficient use of nuclear energy.

Railroads are constantly exploring exciting possibilities like this. Such progressive thinking is important to all of us — for we're going to need railroads more than ever in the boom years ahead.

Clearly, it's in the national interest to give railroads equal opportunity and treatment with other forms of transportation. America's railroads — the lifeline of the nation — are the main line to *your* future.

ASSOCIATION OF
AMERICAN RAILROADS
WASHINGTON 6, D. C.

There was optimism about nuclear fission at the dawn of the nuclear age, shown in this 1948 Association of American Railroads print advertisement. *Association of American Railroads*

race, and then concluded his remarks by calling for the formation of an International Atomic Energy Agency to regulate and promote the worldwide development of civilian nuclear power.

While the efficacy of actively sharing nuclear know-how, materials, and technology with other countries was questionable, few Americans doubted the application of nuclear energy for civilian purposes in the United States. In fact, there was excitement about the prospects. Nuclear power would soon be used in Navy submarines, on surface ships, and for generating electricity. Why not atomic cars, planes, and trains? After all, why not an atomic locomotive?

Dr. Lyle Borst's atomic locomotive proposal

While the idea of an atomic-powered locomotive was in the air at least as early as 1946,[266] Dr. Borst's atomic locomotive proposal emerged on January 1, 1954, less than a month after Eisenhower's "Atoms for Peace" speech. Then, Borst and his students issued their report, "An Atomic Locomotive – A Feasibility Study."[267]

This was the same Borst who testified before the U.S. Congress

that he co-founded the Federation of Atomic Scientists in order "to create a realization of the dangers that this nation and all civilization will face if the tremendous destructive potential of nuclear energy is misused."[268]

The atomic locomotive that Borst and his students envisioned would have used a small nuclear reactor as its energy source. The heat generated by the fissioning of uranium-235 in this reactor would boil water to make steam, which would be fed into a steam turbine. The turbine shaft would turn generators to produce electricity for the locomotive's electric traction motors. Thus, this locomotive would be categorized as an Atomic STEL.

The proposed atomic locomotive was also called the A-locomotive,[269] the Atom Burner,[270] and the X-12. The latter name was presumably because the locomotive would have been experimental with 12 traction motors driving 12 axles. The X-12 would have been another giant two-unit locomotive, stretching 160 feet in length.

According to various artists' renditions, the front of the 100-foot-long lead unit would have looked like an EMD F-type or an Alco PA diesel-electric locomotive. Halfway down its side there would have been a large square shape, which outlined the nuclear reactor's radiation shielding.

The reactor itself was described as having internal dimensions of just 3 x 3 x 1 feet. A 4-foot-thick radiation shield weighing 250 tons would have been wrapped around it. Thus, the weight of just its radiation shielding would have exceeded the weight of an entire modern GE ES44AC or EMD SD70ACe locomotive.

In addition to the reactor and its shielding, the locomotive's lead unit would've contained the steam turbine, a steam condenser, electric generators, and electric traction motors.

The 60-foot second unit would've carried radiators and fans for cooling and water recovery purposes. This locomotive would have produced large amounts of heat that would need to be dissipated into the atmosphere.

An aqueous homogenous reactor

was chosen for this project because information about it was in the public domain and it had already been tested by Los Alamos Laboratory. This type of reactor uses liquid uranium fuel mixed with water that serves as the reactor's moderator (slowing neutrons to permit fission) and its coolant (removing heat to make steam and to prevent overheating).

Borst's initial feasibility study describes the steam turbine as 25% efficient "according to the steam tables."[271] However, according to Borst, the reactor was designed to produce an output of 30 Megawatts (MW) of heat for the steam turbine in the form of 250 psi steam, while the locomotive's steam turbine shaft output would have been 8,000 horsepower.[272] Based on these figures—the energy input and output of the steam turbine—the turbine's efficiency can be calculated to be 19.9%.

Turbine Energy Input = 30 MW
Turbine Energy Output = 8,000 horsepower

1 horsepower = 0.746 kilowatts (KW)
Therefore 8,000 hp = 8,000 hp x 0.746 KW/hp = 5,968 KW = 5.968 MW

$$\text{Efficiency} = \frac{5.968 \text{ MW}}{30 \text{ MW}} = 0.1989 \text{ or } 19.9\%$$

According to Borst, X-12 would have 7,200 horsepower "available for traction purposes," i.e. gear-reduced shaft power delivered to traction generators for the purpose of generating electricity to propel the locomotive.[273]

From this, we know that 800 horsepower would've been consumed by the A-locomotive's auxiliaries, the latter being the pumps, fans, compressors, and every other piece of energy-consuming equipment other than the traction generator and traction motors. This auxiliaries' horsepower value is large, but not necessarily unexpected given the A-locomotive's cooling requirements.

However, Borst's description of his atomic locomotive varied. For

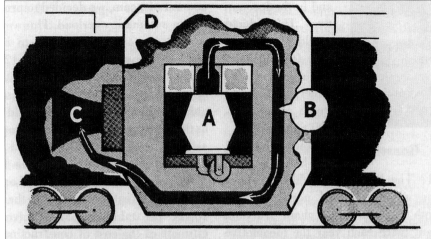

THE SOURCE OF POWER

A cutaway section shows basic principle of the proposed atomic locomotive. The nuclear reactor (A), containing a solution of uranium 235 would produce steam which would pass through pipes (B) to steam turbine (C). This turbine would drive four direct current generators producing the electricity to propel the locomotive. A 500,000 lb. steel block four feet thick (D) would protect the crew from radiation

This image from the June 1954 issue of *Railway Progress* gives a schematic view of the reactor and turbine. *Railway Progress*

example, in another place he remarked that his locomotive would produce 7,000 horsepower "at the rails."[274] To accomplish that, the amount of power delivered to the generators for traction purposes would need to be around 8,500 horsepower. This and other inconsistencies were probably the result of Borst's proposal evolving over time.

The steam turbine's high speed would have been reduced by a gear box connected to four 1.3 MW generators. In order to fit all of this into the space available in the locomotive, Borst believed the generators would have to be long and narrow in a shape—a configuration not yet invented.

Borst envisioned that his locomotive's electric traction motors would occasionally operate at an output in excess of their continuous rating.[275] He said they could do this because they were, after all, powered by "an 'infinite' or unlimited power source."[276] By this he did not mean God or an electric catenary (as in the case of the electric locomotive), but by an atomic reactor!

The X-12's braking would be accomplished conventionally. Like a diesel-electric locomotive, the atomic locomotive would utilize dynamic brakes using electric traction motors to provide retarding force by functioning as generators. The electricity the motors produced would be dissipated into the atmosphere by electric resistance grids located within the locomotive. Those grids would be cooled by fans.

The economics of the X-12

While Borst and his students may have enjoyed the technical details of the atomic locomotive (and the challenge of squeezing a nuclear power plant into a locomotive), the professor knew that railroad companies would never be interested in such a locomotive unless it would cost less than other motive power options. Thus, the X-12 proposal included an economic analysis that was intended to show how an atomic locomotive could be more cost-effective than a diesel-electric locomotive. Conventional steam locomotives were on their way out at the time, being replaced by diesels.

Borst estimated the cost of the X-12 to be $1.2 million ($11 million in 2018 dollars) compared to the $596,000 cost of purchasing four diesel-electric locomotives at the time.[277] Why four diesels? That's how many would be needed to match the horsepower of the single atomic locomotive. In order for the atomic locomotive to be cost-competitive, its $604,000 premium purchase price ($1.2 million minus $596,000 = $604,000) would have to be overcome by reduced fuel costs and lower maintenance and operating costs.

The physicist probably significantly underestimated the maintenance costs of his locomotive when he equated them to those of the four diesels. Moreover, even if uranium fuel per unit of energy was less expensive than diesel fuel, refueling an atomic locomotive would have been much more complicated, difficult, risky, and expensive than refueling a diesel-electric locomotive.

It would've required, after all, a specially built facility with highly trained non-railroad staff. It would have also needed a repository or reprocessing facility for spent nuclear fuel with sufficient security to prevent diversion of this potentially very dangerous material. As was representative of the era, the issue and costs of radioactive waste disposal were not addressed. Accident risk was downplayed and insurance costs probably unaddressed. After all, what could possibly go wrong?

Public relations and the final outcome

What started as an academic exercise became a public relations campaign as Borst championed the idea of an atomic locomotive to an interested industry and public. In an article published in 1954 in *Railway Progress*, Borst stated that "Babcock & Wilcox Co. (the presumed locomotive builder) is undertaking engineering design studies and making laboratory tests looking toward a complete design and eventual construction of the A-locomotive."[278] In this same article he argued that oil and coal reserves would be depleted before long, making a locomotive powered by splitting

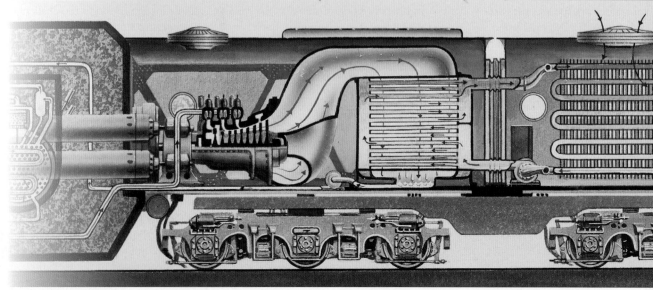

atoms "look mighty good to the railroads."

While the idea of building an atomic locomotive may seem farfetched now, apparently it was easy to get caught up in the moment in the 1950s, as evidenced by *Popular Science*, *Life*, and *Trains* magazines. An optimistic April 1954 *Popular Science* article on the X-12 predicted that there was "a reasonable chance" the locomotive would be built. *Life* magazine's June 21, 1954, two-page spread on the X-12 described the locomotive as a "physics professor's practical dream," implying that it could and might be built. And the editors of *Trains* magazine gave contributing author Edward J. Kehoe's

July 1955 article a subtitle describing atomic power as "the next revolution in (locomotive) motive power."[279] Kehoe concluded that, "Based on the rapid progress of reactor technology, the railroads can have their first atomic locomotive in operation in 1960, if they want to!"

Thankfully they did not.

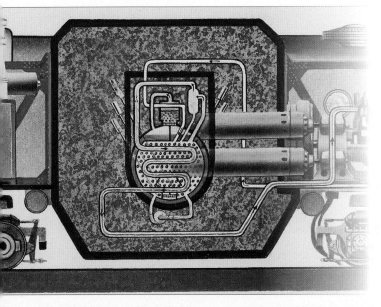

Dr. Lyle Borst's atomic locomotive as depicted by commercial artist and illustrator Rolf Klep. Klep's work was featured in many magazines from 1927 to 1956. This image appeared as a two-page spread in the July 21, 1954, edition of *Life* magazine. Accompanying text states that the locomotive could travel twice around the world without refueling. The illustration shows the nuclear reactor, steam turbine, electric generators (two as-yet un-invented cylindrical generators), and condenser. Heat rejection from this locomotive would be substantial enough to require a 65-foot radiator car just to cool the water that picked up heat in the condenser.
"Atomic Locomotive," 1954, Rolf Klep, Watercolor and gouache on board. Gift of Rolf Klep, Jordan Schnitzer Museum of Art, University of Oregon, 1987:535

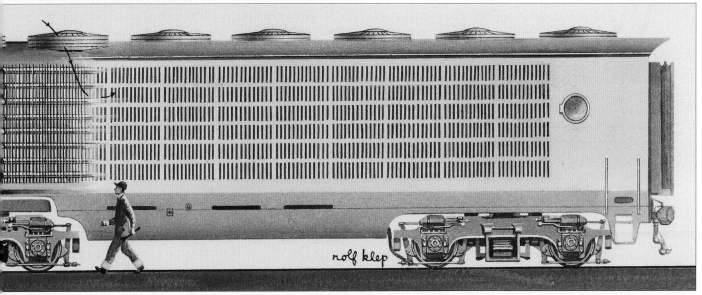

5

The future of turbine-powered locomotives and trains

While future steam turbine motive power is unlikely, locomotives with gas turbine prime movers might see future action on American and Canadian railroads, though in very limited numbers at best. It's easy to see that the deck is stacked against gas turbine motive power. Consider these barriers:

- The performance, fuel economy, market dominance, and success of diesel-electric locomotives
- Railroad industry practice to rebuild and reuse old locomotives, reducing the need for new locomotives
- Requirement that locomotives operate interchangeably between railroads cross-country

- The high cost of turbine locomotives and trains, especially when built as single locomotives or in small numbers
- Inferior fuel economy of gas turbines, especially at part-load and when idling
- High maintenance costs of non-standardized turbine locomotives requiring special repair facilities and maintenance staff training
- Additional refueling infrastructure costs if a fuel other than diesel fuel is used, such as natural gas
- Impossibility of predicting future alternative fuel costs and their price differential with diesel fuel
- Risk-averse nature of the railroad industry

The above notwithstanding, the proponents of gas turbine motive power can point to promising developments, such as microturbine engines that deliver greater fuel economy at lower cost. These heavy-haul engines incorporate ceramic components to permit higher combustion temperatures and variable geometry nozzles that increase part-load efficiency.

A compact recuperator is used to recover exhaust heat for combustion air preheating and an intercooler may be incorporated to improve the efficiency of a two-stage air compressor. The efficiency of these gas turbine engines is now above 40% with further improvements expected. Their simple design suggests that they can be built

Turbine-powered locomotives and trains, such as the Alco/General Electric prototype that convinced Union Pacific to invest in the technology in the 1950s, have been set aside by the railroad industry, perhaps forever, perhaps just for the time being. *General Electric*

by truck turbocharger manufacturers.

But these microturbines produce only 400 to 500 horsepower. Ten of them would be required for a line-haul locomotive. Multiple small turbines could be accommodated in a genset-type configuration. This would allow individual turbines to be switched on and off to match load on an as-needed basis. Thus, all but one operating turbine could be running at full load and maximum efficiency.

The addition of batteries could further improve turbine operating efficiency while potentially also permitting regenerative braking and full hybrid locomotive operation (if the batteries were large enough).

However intriguing, this concept would probably be resisted by railroads that have also rejected the genset concept, which at present is most railroads. Even if these turbine engines were highly reliable and a locomotive's modular nature facilitated quick engine swaps, railroads do not want to maintain 10 engines per locomotive.

The previously discussed CINGL concept offers a number of insights about how to make gas turbine locomotives cost-effective. The CINGL proposal consisted of a gas turbine locomotive that burned compressed natural gas. It was to have operated in captive service, along one route operated by the same railroad. This strategy avoided the issue of interoperability with other railroads, making it possible to refuel and maintain a small fleet of gas turbine locomotives at a reasonable infrastructure cost.[280]

To improve the CINGL's fuel economy, the locomotive was to be paired with one or more companion diesel-electric locomotives (to handle part-load operation) while operating it on an uncongested route to permit as much full-load turbine operation as possible. Moreover, the CINGL carried its own CNG fuel, thus avoiding the need for a fuel tender and associated additional capital and operational costs.

While the CINGL concept provides a model for reintroducing gas turbine locomotives in the future, one of its key features—its use of natural gas—is also its Achilles' heel. It's true that when natural gas is burned, it produces less "criteria pollutants" (i.e. nitrogen oxides, particulates, hydrocarbons, and carbon monoxide) and carbon dioxide. This desirable "burner tip" performance gave natural gas its green image.

But now an increasing amount of natural gas is produced by hydraulic fracturing or "fracking," which has many negative environmental impacts.[281] And methane leakage during the production of natural gas (natural gas is primarily methane) may actually give this fuel a greater global warming impact than diesel fuel.[282] In an era of accelerating climate change, switching from diesel fuel to natural gas is not a sustainable solution.

Climate change will force railroads and all sectors of the economy to rethink fossil fuels, prompting significant reductions in their use and then wholesale transition to energy sources that don't emit greenhouse gases. Thus, if there are gas turbine-powered locomotives and trains in the future, they would ideally be much more energy efficient throughout their output range and fired or co-fired by sustainable fuels. These fuels could be biofuel or hydrogen produced with minimal or no fossil fuels.

While turbine-powered locomotives and trains occupy only a small corner of American railroad history, their unique stories are intriguing and worth retelling. In challenging the dominant diesel engine, some fared better than others. Hopefully, this retrospective has done justice to these remarkable and fascinating machines.

RESOURCES FOR FURTHER READING AND STUDY

Most of the following references were published years ago. Interested readers can still find these documents through online searches, on eBay, with the help of railroad historical societies, at libraries, or through interlibrary loan, especially with the help of a research librarian. Internet resources were available at the time this book was published.

The resources are broken down as follows:

• General references about turbine power or turbine-powered locomotives, including references about more than one type of turbine locomotive
• References about each specific type of turbine locomotive discussed in this book
• Some relevant websites

Resources are listed title first for ease of use.

Wikipedia and YouTube are also excellent sources of information about these turbine locomotives. YouTube videos are not listed here (with a few exceptions) but can easily be found by searching YouTube.

"STEL" refers to steam turbine electric locomotive and "GTEL" refers to gas turbine electric locomotive.

Resources about Turbine Locomotives in General or about More than One Type of Turbine Locomotive

American Steam Locomotives: Design and Development, 1880 – 1960, William L. Withuhn (Indiana University Press, Bloomington, IN), 2019. For detailed discussions of the UP Bunker fuel-fired STEL, the PRR S2, and the N&W Jawn Henry, see chapter 21, "Resisting the Revolution," pages 402-421.

C&O Power, Eugene L. Huddleston and Alvin Staufer, 1965, pages 298-305.

"Coal-Burning Gas Turbine-Electric Locomotive," Thomas R. Lee, *The Streamliner, Volume 16, No. 4* (Fall 2002). The Streamliner is a publication of the Union Pacific Historical Society.

"Diesel Engines or Gas Turbines for Locomotives: A Review of Current Motive-Power Development," N. C. Dezendorf (Director of Sales, GM Electro-Motive Division), paper presented at the 7th Pan-American Railway Congress, Mexico City, October 10-20, 1950.

Diesel Victory, special edition of *Classic Trains* (Kalmbach Publishing, Waukesha, WI, 2006).

"Economic Assessment of Coal Burning Locomotives," General Electric Company, U.S. Department of Energy report (contract number DE-AC21-85MC22181), 1986.

"Four Turbo-Locomotives That Were Built by Baldwin-Westinghouse and What Went Wrong," James O. Stephens and C.E. Knight, 1993 IEEE/ASMA Railroad Conference Proceedings, April 6, 1993.

"Gas Turbine Locomotive," John L. Yellott and Charles F. Kotteamp, paper presented to Railway Fuel and Traveling Engineers' Association, Chicago, September 6, 1946 (originally published in *Railway Mechanical Engineer*, November 1956 and reprinted in *Train Shed Cyclopedia No. 66*, pages 615-620). Other articles with the same title, published and reprinted as above, but with different authors, are "The Gas-Turbine Locomotive" by Paul Sidler and "Gas Turbine Locomotives" by Walter Giger.

GE and EMD Locomotives, Brian Solomon (Voyager Press, Minneapolis, MN, 2014), 58-67.

"More Power on Wheels: Diesel, Steam or Turbine, A Huskier Iron Horse Emerges from a Quiet Revolution of Railroading," Devon Francis, *Popular Science*, October 1946, pages 66-72.

N&W: Giant of Steam, Major Lewis Ingles Jeffries (Pruett Publishing Company, Boulder CO, 1980). See section on "Proposed and Experimental" locomotives, pages 274-285.

"New York Central Coal Turbines!," *Central Headlight*, New York Central System Historical Society, Fourth Quarter, 1981.

"Postwar Parade: 2," A.C. Kalmbach, *Trains*, November 1945. (The article is about gas turbine locomotives.)

A Practical Evaluation of Railroad Motive Power, P.W. Kiefer, Steam Locomotive Research Institute, NY, 1947.

Railroad and Locomotive Technology Roadmap (ANL/ESD/02-6), Center for Transportation Research Argonne National Laboratory, U.S. Department of Energy, 2002.

"Story of Turbine Locomotives," Michael A. Eagleton, *Railroad* magazine, February 1970, pages 18-25.

"Turbine Locomotives," www.classicstreamliners.com/lo-turbines.html.

"Turbines: King Coal Battles the Diesel," Erik Hirsimaki, *Classic Trains* (Kalmbach Publishing, Waukesha, WI, Fall 2004).

Turbines Westward, Thomas R. Lee (T. Lee Publications, Clay Center, Kansas, 1975).

Turbotrains International, Wolfgang Stoffels (Birkhäuser, Basel/Boston, 1983). This book is written in German but there is a hard-to-find English edition.

"*Union Pacific's Mighty Turbines*" DVD produced by the Union Pacific Historical Society, available from www.pentrex.com.

"What Type Motive Power," H.E.

Dralle, *Railway Age*, January 1, 1949.

The World's Fastest Trains – From the Age of Steam to the TGV, Geoffrey Freemen Allen (Ian Allan Ltd/Patrick Stephens Limited, 1978 and 1992).

How a Steam Locomotive Works, Karen Parker (TLC Publishing, Forest, VA, 2008). This book does not discuss turbine locomotives but is an excellent reference on the conventional reciprocating coal-fired steam locomotives many turbines were intended to replace.

Union Pacific STEL

American Steam Locomotives: Design and Development, 1880 – 1960, William L. Withuhn (Indiana University Press, Bloomington, IN), 2019. For discussion of UP STEL, see chapter 21, "Resisting the Revolution," pages 403-408.

GE and EMD Locomotives, Brian Solomon (Voyager Press, Minneapolis, MN, 2014), pages 59-63.

"Steam-Electric Locomotive Is Ready to OUTSPEED All Its Rivals," Stanley A. Dennis, *Science and Mechanics*, April 1939.

"The Steam Turbine-Electric Story," Thomas R. Lee, *The Streamliner, Volume 10, No. 2* (1995). The Streamliner is a publication of the Union Pacific Historical Society.

"Turbines: King Coal Battles the Diesel," Erik Hirsimaki, *Classic Trains* (Kalmbach Publishing, Waukesha, WI, Fall 2004).

Turbines Westward, Thomas R. Lee (T. Lee Publications, Clay Center, Kansas, 1975).

"*Union Pacific's Mighty Turbines*" DVD produced by the Union Pacific Historical Society, available from www.pentrex.com.

Pennsylvania Railroad S2 Direct Drive Steam Turbine Locomotive

American Steam Locomotives: Design and Development, 1880 – 1960, William L. Withuhn (Indiana University Press, Bloomington, IN), 2019. For discussion of PRR S2, see chapter 21, "Resisting the Revolution," pages 408-411.

"Driving Gear for Turbine Locomotive," *Trains*, June 1945.

"Four Turbo-Locomotives That Were Built by Baldwin-Westinghouse and What Went Wrong," James O. Stephens and C.E. Knight, 1993 IEEE/ASMA Railroad Conference Proceedings, April 6, 1993.

Pennsy Power: Steam and Electric Locomotives of the Pennsylvania Railroad, 1900-1957, Alvin F. Staufer, 1962, pages 240 – 243 (S2 direct drive steam turbine locomotive).

"The Pennsylvania Geared Turbine Locomotive," J.S. Newton and W.A. Brecht, *The Railway Mechanical Engineer*, March 1945. (Train Shed Cyclopedia No. 56).

"Pennsylvania's Turbine Engine," *Trains*, January 1945.

"The Pennsy's Mighty Turbine – Battleship on Rails," Preston Cook, *Classic Trains* (Kalmbach Publishing, Waukesha, WI, Spring 2012).

"Problems with the Operation of the S2," David E. Slee, *The Keystone*, Spring 2013, pages 33-41. In this same issue of *The Keystone* also see "Thoughts on Neil Burnell's S2 Article," David Evans, pages 32-33. *The Keystone* is the quarterly publication of the PRR Technical and Historical Society.

"The Steam Turbine: Coal's New Hope," Charles Kerr Jr., *Trains*, June 1947, pages 14-18.

"Steam Turbine Locomotive," *Baldwin* (quarterly magazine of the Baldwin Locomotive Works), Fourth Quarter 1944, pages 4-14.

"Test Run of S2 #6200," M. E. Brown, *The Keystone*, Spring 2001, pages 60-61. The Keystone is the quarterly publication of the PRR Technical and Historical Society.

"The Trials and Tribulations of #6200," Neil Burnell, *The Keystone*, Autumn 2012, page 36. Also, same issue of The Keystone, "Test Run of the #6200," M.E. Brown, page 57. #6200 was the Pennsylvania Railroad's direct drive steam turbine locomotive. The Keystone is the quarterly publication of the PRR Technical and Historical Society.

"Turbine Locomotives," www.classicstreamliners.com/lo-turbines.html.

"Turbines: King Coal Battles the Diesel," Erik Hirsimaki, *Classic Trains* (Kalmbach Publishing, Waukesha, WI, Fall 2004).

"Turbine Power," David Jackson, *The Keystone*, Summer 1995, pages 23-39. In this same issue are sidebars about the S2 by T.J. Putz and F.L. Alben of the Westinghouse Corporation; Roger L. Keyser; William M. Moedinger; and Chuck Blardone.

Pennsylvania Railroad's Triplex Locomotive Design Concept

N&W: Giant of Steam, Major Lewis Ingles Jeffries (Pruett Publishing Company, Boulder, CO, 1980). See section on "Proposed and Experimental" locomotives, page 278.

"Proposed Design of a 4-8-4-8 Freight Locomotive," Pennsylvania Railroad, April 27, 1944, which is available from the Norfolk & Western Historical Society as their document HOL-00872.07.01.

Train Talks, Pennsylvania Railroad, April 1945, a copy of which is included in *Rails Remembered: Volume 4 – The Tale of the Turbine*, Louis M. Newton, self-published, 2002, pages 714-716 (available from the Norfolk and Western Historical Society).

Chesapeake & Ohio M-1 STEL

American Steam Locomotives: Design and Development, 1880 – 1960, William L. Withuhn (Indiana University Press, Bloomington, IN), 2019. For discussion of C&O M-1 STEL, see chapter 21, "Resisting the Revolution," pages 411-414.

C&O Power, Eugene L. Huddleston and Alvin Staufer, 1965, pages 298-305.

"C&O's Steam Turbine Locomotives," *Trains*, (Kalmbach Publishing, Waukesha, WI), February 1971, pages 47-49

"Four Turbo-Locomotives That Were Built by Baldwin-Westinghouse and What Went Wrong," James O. Stephens and C.E. Knight, 1993 IEEE/ASMA Railroad Conference Proceedings, April 6, 1993.

"The Genesis, Design, and Performance of C&O's Steam-Turbo-Electric Class M-1, Part I," Gene Huddleston, *C&O Historical Magazine* (Chesapeake & Ohio Historical Society), September 1997.

"The Genesis, Design, and Performance of C&O's Steam-Turbo-Electric Class M-1, Part 2," Gene Huddleston, *C&O Historical Magazine* (Chesapeake & Ohio Historical Society), October 1997.

"The Genesis, Design, and Performance of C&O's Steam-Turbo-Electric Class M-1," Gene Huddleston, *National Railway Bulletin*, Volume 68, Number 5, 2003 (National Railway Historical Society), pages 20-42.

The Locomotives that Baldwin Built, Fred Westing (Bonanza Books, New York, 1966), pages 187-188.

"This Was the Train That Was (But Never Was)," Geoffrey H. George, Trains, July 1968, pages 38-47.

"Turbines: King Coal Battles the Diesel," Erik Hirsimaki, *Classic Trains* (Kalmbach Publishing, Waukesha, WI, Fall 2004).

Norfolk & Western TE-1 #2300 STEL

American Steam Locomotives: Design and Development, 1880 – 1960, William L. Withuhn (Indiana University Press, Bloomington, IN), 2019. For discussion of N&W TE-1, see chapter 21, "Resisting the Revolution," pages 414-417.

"Ask Trains," *Trains*, August 2007.

"Baldwin Locomotive Works, Specification No. 48-D-18 of a Baldwin Locomotive Works, Westinghouse Electric Corporation, Babcock & Wilcox Company 4500 Horsepower Coal-Fired Steam Turbine Electric Drive Locomotive with Tender" for Norfolk & Western Railway Company, December 15, 1948 (available from the Norfolk & Western Historical Society as their document HOL-00872.07.02).

"Four Turbo-Locomotives That Were Built by Baldwin-Westinghouse and What Went Wrong," James O. Stephens and C.E. Knight, 1993 IEEE/ASMA Railroad Conference Proceedings, April 6, 1993.

"Is This the Last Stand of the Iron Horse," Walton M. Rock, *Popular Mechanics*, January 1955, pages 83-87.

The Locomotives that Baldwin Built, Fred Westing (Bonanza Books, New York, 1966), page 191.

"Mallets to Jawn Henry," C.E. Pond, *Trains*, October 1984, pages 44-45. C.E. Pond was General Manager for Motive Power & Equipment, Norfolk & Western, 1953-1967.

N&W Gets Steam Turbine Locomotive, *Modern Railroads*, July 1954.

N&W: Giant of Steam, Major Lewis Ingles Jeffries (Pruett Publishing Company, Boulder, CO, 1980). See section on "Proposed and Experimental" locomotives, pages 282 - 285.

"Operator's Manual—Steam Turbine Electric Freight Locomotive with Dynamic Braking," Norfolk and Western Railroad No. 2300, Baldwin-Lima-Hamilton Corporation, Philadelphia, PA, September 1953.

Rails Remembered: Volume 4—The Tale of a Turbine, Louis M. Newton, 2002. Available from the Norfolk & Western Historical Society.

"Turbines: King Coal Battles the Diesel," Erik Hirsimaki, *Classic Trains* (Kalmbach Publishing, Waukesha, WI, Fall 2004).

Union Pacific Fuel Oil-Fired GTEL

"101: Gas Turbine," *Trains*, July 1949.

Big Blows: Union Pacific's Super Turbines, Harold Keekley (George R. Cockle & Associates, Omaha, NE, 1975).

"Diesel and Turbine Test on the Wasatch Grade in the Early 1950s," Mark Amfahr, *The Streamliner, Vol. 28, No 2* (Spring 2014). The Streamliner is a publication of the Union Pacific Historical Society.

"Evaluation of the Gas Turbine Electric Locomotive," Gibbs & Hill Consulting Engineers, March 27, 1953.

"First Gas Electric Locomotive," *Mechanix Illustrated*, July 1950, Pages 80-81.

"The Gas Turbine Electric Locomotive Story," David I. Smith, 1986 (unpublished paper written for the Senior Erie Elfun Society Historical Project.

"Horsepower Without Cylinders," David P. Morgan, *Trains*, March 1956.

"I Rode 'Big Blow'," Wallace W. Abbey, *Trains*, July 1953.

"Oil Burning Gas Turbine Locomotives," G.M. Davies (Locomotive Editor), *1966 Car and Locomotive Cyclopedia* (Simmons Boardman Publishing, New York, NY 1966), page 1061.

"Operation of 8500-Hp Gas Turbines in Locomotive Service," H. Rees (Union Pacific Railroad), presented at Gas Turbine Power Conference, American Society of Mechanical Engineers, Washington, DC, March 5-9, 1961, ASME paper 61-GTP-8. (This paper focuses on maintenance and repair issues associated with the first group of 8,500 hp gas turbine locomotives.)

"The Propane Gas Turbine Research Project," Thomas R. Lee, *The Streamliner*, Summer 1994, pages 26-37.

"Turbines Across the Desert," Gordon Glattenberg, *Classic Trains*, Summer 2010, pages 22-27.

"Turbines: King Coal Battles the Diesel," Erik Hirsimaki, *Classic Trains* (Kalmbach Publishing, Waukesha, WI, Fall 2004).

"Turbine Locomotives," www.classicstreamliners.com/lo-turbines.html.

Turbines Westward, Thomas R. Lee (T. Lee Publications, Clay Center, Kansas, 1975).

"Union Pacific's Mighty Turbines" DVD produced by the Union Pacific Historical Society, available from www.pentrex.com.

Westinghouse-Baldwin Fuel Oil-Fired "Blue Goose" GTEL

"4000-hp Gas Turbines Passenger Locomotives," W.A. Brecht, Charles Kerr, Jr.; T.J. Putz, *Railway Mechanical and Electrical Engineer*, January 1950 (available in *Train Shed Cyclopedia, No.80*).

"A 4,000 hp Gas Turbine Locomotive for Passenger Service," W.A. Brecht, Charles Kerr, Jr.; T.J. Putz, presented at the annual meeting of the American Society of Mechanical Engineers, November 27-December 2, 1949.

"Four Turbo-Locomotives That Were Built by Baldwin-Westinghouse and What Went Wrong," James O. Stephens and C.E. Knight, 1993 IEEE/ASMA Railroad Conference Proceedings, April 6, 1993.

"The Gas Turbine as Railroad Motive Power," J. K. Hodnette (Vice President, Westinghouse Corporation) November 12, 1952, luncheon address, Chicago, IL, following inspection of the Blue Goose by railroad officials.

"Operating Record of the Westinghouse-Baldwin Gas Turbine Locomotive," Charles Kerr, Jr., T.J. Putz, and T.L. Weybrew (all of the Westinghouse Corporation), presented at the annual meeting of the American Society of Mechanical Engineers, November 30-December 5, 1952.

"Progress Report—Baldwin-Westinghouse Gas-Turbine Electric Locomotive," T.J. Putz (Manager, Locomotive and Gas Turbine Engineering Division, Westinghouse Corp.), Power Engineering, November 1951.

"Thrifty Glutton," David Morgan, *Trains*, January 1953.

"Turbine Locomotives," www.classicstreamliners.com/lo-turbines.html.

Turbines Westward, Thomas R. Lee (T. Lee Publications, Clay Center, Kansas, 1975).

"Westinghouse Gas-Turbine Locomotive," (no author listed), *Diesel Railway Traction*, June, 1954, pages 142-145.

"What Type Motive Power," H.E. Dralle, *Railway Age*, January 1, 1949.

Union Pacific Coal-Fired GTEL

"Another Turbine Hits the Trail," David P. Morgan, *Trains*, March 1963.

"Coal-Burning Gas Turbine-Electric Locomotive," Thomas R. Lee, *The Streamliner, Volume 16, No. 4* (Fall 2002). The Streamliner is a publication of the Union Pacific Historical Society.

"Coal Burning Gas Turbine Locomotive," G.M. Davies (Locomotive Editor), *1966 Car and Locomotive Cyclopedia* (Simmons Boardman Publications, NY, 1966), pages 1058-1059.

GE and EMD Locomotives, Brian Solomon (Voyager Press, Minneapolis, MN, 2014), pages 63-67.

"Turbines: King Coal Battles the Diesel," Erik Hirsimaki, *Classic Trains* (Kalmbach Publishing, Waukesha, WI, Fall 2004).

"Turbine Locomotives," www.classicstreamliners.com/lo-turbines.html.

Turbines Westward, Thomas R. Lee (T. Lee Publications, Clay Center, Kansas, 1975).

"Union Pacific's Mighty Turbines" DVD produced by the Union Pacific Historical Society, available from www.pentrex.com.

The Quest for a Viable Coal-Burning GTEL

"ALCO-GE Gas Turbine-Electric Completes Preliminary Tests," *Railway Age*, June 18, 1949, page 85.

"Coal-Burning Gas Turbine-Electric Locomotive" in the Union Pacific Historical Society's *The Streamliner, Volume 16, No. 4* (Fall 2002).

"Coal-Fired Gas Turbine for Locomotive Propulsion," Leon Green, Jr., Energy Conversion Alternatives, Ldt., ASME 87-GT-273, 1987.

"Comparison of the Freight Motive Power Operating Costs Prepared for the Locomotive Development Committee of Bituminous Coal Research, Inc.," J. I. Yellow and P.R. Broadley, July 1, 1952. (Available from the Norfolk & Western Historical Society their document HOL-00872.10).

"Design of Advanced Coal-Fired Gas Turbine Locomotives," Sidney G. Liddle, California Engineering Research Institute, ASME 85-IGT-48, 1985.

"Future Fuels and Engines for Railroad Locomotives," S.G. Liddle et. al., Jet Propulsion Laboratory, California Institute of Technology (prepared for the U.S. Department of Energy), November 1, 1981.

"Gas Turbine Locomotive," John L. Yellott and Charles F. Kotteamp, from a paper presented to Railway Fuel and Traveling Engineers' Association, Chicago, September 6, 1946 (*Train Shed Cyclopedia No. 66*, pages 615-620).

"Gas Turbine Power," W. Giger, Railway Mechanical Engineer, October 1948, page 92 (574). This is an abstract of a paper

presented to the Power Division of the American Society of Mechanical Engineers, Portland, OR, September 7-9, 1948 (*Train Shed Cyclopedia No. 80*).

New York Central M-497 Jet-Powered Budd Rail Car

The Flight of the M-497: The Story of New York Central's Record-Setting Speed Trials, Hank Morris with Don Wetzel, 2007. Available through www.lulu.com.

NY Metropolitan Transportation Authority Gas Turbine Commuter Cars

"Car in L.I.R.R. Test Develops Gas Pains," *New York Times*, April 12, 1970.

"Dual-Powered Gas Turbine/Electric Commuter Rail Cars: Test, Evaluations, and Economics," Donald Raskin, Charles Stark, and L.T. Klauder & Associates (prepared for the New York Metropolitan Transportation Authority under the sponsorship of the U.S. Urban Mass Transportation Authority, USDOT), September 1980. This report is available by interlibrary loan. The author's research librarian obtained a copy from the Northwestern University Library.

"GT-2 Test Car Undergoing Daily Runs on Long Island Tracks for High Speed Commuter Service," NY Metropolitan Transportation Authority press release, July 29, 1970.

"Here's an Invitation for a Turbine Ride," *Long Island Railroader*, September 22, 1966.

"L.I.R.R Awaiting Gas-Turbine Cars," Edward C. Burks, *New York Times*, January 26, 1975.

"LIRR GT 1/2 Gas Turbine Cars," from the, "gas turbine cars" section of www.trainsarefun.com website.

Penn Central/Amtrak UAC TurboTrain

"CN Turbotrain—3:59—The Lost Film," YouTube video.

"CN Turbotrain Part 1, 2, and 3 1970," Canadian National promotional YouTube video.

"The Fading Days of the Turbo," El Simon, Jr., *Passenger Train Journal*, July 1996, pages 32-39.

"Second Chance for Turbo," William D. Middleton, *Trains*, June 1971, pages 29-30.

"An Objectivity Test," David P. Morgan, *Trains*, November 1968, pages 26-29.

"Train 153: A Trip on a Turbo," Benjamin B. Bachman, *Trains*, page 42-45.

"Turbine Locomotives," www.classicstreamliners.com/lo-turbines.html.

"TurboTrain," Sikorsky Product History, www.sikorskyarchives.com/Turbo_Train.php.

TURBOTRAIN: A Journey, Jason Shron, Rapido Trains Inc., 2007.

"TURBOTRAIN: Can It Put Profit in

Passengers," F.N. Houser, *Railway Age*, June 19, 1967.

"TURBOTRAIN," Is the Hardware Equal to the Hard Sell?," Harold A. Edmonson, *Trains*, April 1969.

"Turbotrain Revisited," William D. Middleton, *Trains*, March 1970, pages 32-39.

"TurboTrains for the New York Central System," United Aircraft Corporate Systems Center, September 27, 1967.

"The TurboTrain Story," Marc J. Frattasio, *NHRHTA Shoreliner, Volume 29, Issue 2 and 3* (2002).

"United Aircraft's Turbo Train: The Transfer of Aerospace Technology to Rail Transportation," Michael P. Chaney (Railroad History, Railroad & Locomotive Historical Society, Spring 1986).

The World's Fastest Trains – From the Age of Steam to the TGV, Geoffrey Freemen Allen (Ian Allan Ltd/Patrick Stephens Limited, 1978 and 1992), pages 140-143.

Amtrak RTG and RTL Turboliners

"The American Turboliner," Jerome R. Pier, Presented at Gas Turbine and Products Show, Houston, TX, March 2-6, 1975. ASME report 75-GT-108.

"Agreement between the New York State Department of Transportation and the National Railroad Passenger Corporation (Amtrak) for New York State High Speed Rail Program," March 14, 2000. This document was subsequent to a Memorandum of Understanding between the same parties dated September 24, 1998.

"The American Turboliner: A Progress Report," Jerome R. Pier, presented at the Gas Turbine and Aeroengine Congress and Exposition, June 4-8, 1989, Toronto, Canada, ASME report 89-GT-110.

"Americanizing the Turboliner," William D. Middleton, *Railway Age*, April 14, 1975.

"Biggest Travel News Since the 747," David P. Morgan, *Trains*, January 1974.

"Engines of Amtrak—Turboliners," YouTube video.

"The Fading Days of the Turbo," El Simon, Jr., *Passenger Train Journal*, July 1996, pages 32-39.

"Report on the RTL-2 Turboliner High-Speed Demonstration," Federal Railroad Administration, August 9, 1995.

"Report on the Testing of an Upgraded Turbine Trainset," Edward J. Lombardi and Janice P. Li, Mechanical and Engineering Services, Philadelphia, PA, Amtrak, March 10, 1995.

Trail of the Turbo: The Amtrak Turboliner Story, Dale A. Johnson (self-published, 2016, available through Amazon).

"Turbine Locomotives," www.classicstreamliners.com/lo-turbines.html.

"What's New in Amtrak's Roundhouse," Don Phillips, *Trains*, March 1973.

Compressed Integrated Natural Gas Locomotive (GTEL)

"A Concept for a Natural Gas Fueled Locomotive that Uses a Gas Turbine," F.W. Donnelly, SAE Technical Paper Series #891699, presented at Future Transportation Technology Conference and Exposition, Vancouver, B.C. August 7-10, 1989.

"Comparative Economic Assessment of a Natural Gas Fueled Locomotive with On-Board CNG Storage to Diesel and LNG Variants," Frank Donnelly et. al. paper presented at IEEE/ASME Joint Railroad Conference, Baltimore, MD, April 6, 1995 (14 authors from these companies: Applied Power & Propulsion, AlliedSignal Corporation, Allison Engine Company/ Rolls Royce Aerospace Group, BC Rail, and EDO Energy Company).

"Major Study Confirms 'Staggering' 37% Fuel Cost Savings for U.S. Class 1 Railroads Using Compressed Natural Gas Instead of Diesel," Applied Power & Propulsion press release, April 6, 1995.

Bombardier JetTrain GTEL

"ASK TRAINS," *Trains*, January 2009.

"Technology Comparison: High Speed Ground Transportation – Transrapid Superspeed Maglev and Bombardier JetTrain," American Magline Group, December 2002, page 12.

"Turbine Locomotives," www.classicstreamliners.com/lo-turbines.html.

TGV 001 GTEL

"Le Turbotrain Experimental TGV 001," *La Vie du Rail*, April, 1972. (in French)

"Les Essais du TGV 001," *La Vie du Rail*, July 1972. (in French).

"Tests Undertaken with Turbine Train TGV 001," J. Bouley, Proceeding of the Institution of Mechanical Engineers, Volume 191, Issue 1, June 1977.

The World's Fastest Trains – From the Age of Steam to the TGV, Geoffrey Freemen Allen (Ian Allan Ltd/Patrick Stephens Limited, 1978 and 1992), page 155.

Atomic STEL

"The Atomic Locomotive," Lyle Borst and K.W. Petty, *Railway Progress*, July 1954.

"The Atomic Locomotive: A Feasibility Study," Dr. Lyle Borst et.al., Department of Physics, University of Utah, January 1, 1954.

"An Atomic Locomotive Could Be Built," *Popular Science*, April 1954, page 137.

"Dr. Borst's X-12: The Atomic Locomotive," Thornton Waite, *Railroad History #175*, Autumn 1996.

"More Power on Wheels: Diesel, Steam or Turbine, A Huskier Iron Horse Emerges from a Quiet Revolution of Railroading," Devon Francis, *Popular Science*, October 1946, pages 66-72.

"To Peoria by Atom: Atomic Powered-Locomotive," Atomic Skies Blog, Mark J. Appleton, July 2, 2012.

Railroad Historical Societies and Websites

Amtrak – A History of America's Railroad, https://history.amtrak.com.

Chesapeake & Ohio Historical Society, www.cohs.org

National Railway Historical Society, www.nrhs.org

Norfolk & Western Historical Society, www.nwhs.org

Pennsylvania Railroad Technical and Historical Society, www.prrths.com

Union Pacific Historical Society, www.uphs.org

Union Pacific Railroad Museum, www.uprrmuseum.org

Other Websites of Interest

American Rails, www.american-rails.com

Association of American Railroads, www.aar.org

Classic Streamliners, www.classicstreamliners.com

Diesel Era, www.dieselera.com

The Diesel Shop, www.thedieselshop.us

National Association of Railroad Passengers, www.narprail.org

Passenger Train Journal, www.passengertrainjournal.com

Railfan and Railroad, www.railfan.com

Railway Age, www.railwayage.com

Railway Technical Website, www.railway-technical.com

Railway Technology Website, www.railway-technology.com

Trains, trains.com

Amtrak and Class I Railroads

Amtrak, www.amtrak.com

BNSF (Burlington Northern Santa Fe), www.bnsf.com

Canadian National, www.cn.ca

Canadian Pacific, www.cpr.ca

CSX, www.csx.com

Kansas City Southern, www.kcsouthern.com/en-us

Norfolk Southern, www.nscorp.com

Union Pacific, www.up.com

Walter can be reached at www.diesel-electric-locomotives.com, a website created to complement his diesel-electric locomotives book.

Endnotes

These endnotes are deliberately formatted title first (instead of author first) to make them more user-friendly to interested readers who want to dig deeper into the book's various topics.

Most of the references provided in these endnotes were published years ago. Interested readers can still find these documents through online searches, on eBay, at libraries, or through interlibrary loan, especially with the help of a research librarian. Internet resources noted were available at the time this book was published.

1. Dieselization was the transition from reciprocating coal- and oil-burning steam locomotives to diesel fuel-burning diesel-electric locomotives. It started in the late 1930s ran through the 1950s. "How the Diesel Changed Railroading," Jerry A. Pinkepank, *Diesel Victory, Classic Trains* special edition (Kalmbach Publishing), 2006, pages 8-19; and "Why Dieselize," Brian Solomon, *The American Diesel Locomotive*, MBI Publishing Company, 2000, pages 9-17.
2. The locomotive prime mover is its primary source of power. Thus, in diesel-electric locomotives the prime mover is the diesel engine and in turbine-electric locomotives the prime mover is the turbine engine.
3. *Southern Pacific Motive Power Annual 1972*, Joseph A Strapac (Chatham Publishing Company, Burlingame, Calif., 1973), page 12.
4. Ibid.
5. "Union Pacific—Using Bunker C as a Locomotive Fuel," UtahRails.net, utahrails.net/up/bunker-c.php.
6. "Turbine-Driven Locomotive Cuts Coal Consumption in Half," George F. Paul, *Popular Mechanics*, February 1923.
7. "Baldwin/Westinghouse Steam Turbine Locomotive Type 6-8-6" report on Pennsylvania Railroad S2 locomotive test results, Philadelphia, August 12, 1944, Curve No. 5.
8. See 2016 average operating heat rate for coal generating stations, which is given as 10,493 BTU per kilowatt hour (3,412 BTU) or 33%, www.eia.gov/electricity/annual/html/epa_08_01.html.
9. For a discussion of this locomotive, see *Turbines Westward*, Thomas R. Lee, 1975, pages 7-11. For a more comprehensive account, see "The Steam Turbine-Electric Story," also by Thomas Lee, in Volume 10, No. 2 of the Union Pacific Historical Society's *Streamliner* magazine. Also, see "Steam-Electric Locomotive is Ready to OUTSPEED All Its Rivals," Stanley A. Dennis, *Science and Mechanics*, April 1939, and "Union Pacific's Mighty Turbines" DVD produced by the Union Pacific Historical Society, available from www.pentrex.com, as well as the other sources listed in the "Further Reading" section for this locomotive.
10. *Turbines Westward*, pages 7-11.
11. Ibid.
12. See sidebar "Baldwin's Attempt to Market Next-Generation STELs" for explanation of energy benefits on a condensing steam turbine.
13. Ibid., page 7.
14. *GE and EMD Locomotives: The Illustrated History*, Brian Solomon (Voyageur Press, Minneapolis, 2014), page 61.
15. *GE and EMD Locomotives: The Illustrated History*, page 62.
16. For a thorough discussions of the PRR S2 developing, testing, and operation, see *The Keystone, Volume 45, No. 3* (Autumn 2012), Pennsylvania Railroad Technical & Historical Society; and "Battle Ship of the Rails," Preston Cook, *Classic Trains*, Spring 2012.
17. A Belpaire boiler had a squared-off top and was thought by the Pennsylvania Railroad and Baldwin to produce more power than conventional boilers with rounded tops.
18. "Driving Gear for Turbine Locomotive," *Trains*, June 1945, pages 26-29.
19. *The Keystone*, page 52.
20. "The Steam Turbine: Coal's New Hope," Charles Kerr Jr., *Trains*, June 1947, page 15. Kerr reported that the S2 on a special test run pulled 17 passenger cars in excess of 105 mph for 30 miles.
21. "Four Turbo-Locomotives That Were Built by Baldwin-Westinghouse and What Went Wrong," James O. Stephens and C.E. Knight, 1993 IEEE/ASMA Railroad Conference Proceedings, April 6, 1993, pages 17-25.
22. The wheel spinning problem was reduced by adjusting the weight on the principal drivers (the drive wheels on drive axles No. 2 and No. 3), *The Keystone*, page 62.
23. "Four Turbo-Locomotives That Were Built by Baldwin-Westinghouse and What Went Wrong," page 20.
24. P.W. Kiefer, Chief Engineer for Motive Power of the New York Central Railroad, reported that the S2 steam turbine achieved a measured 7,240 shaft horsepower at the PRR Altoona test facility in his "A Practical Evaluation of Railroad Motive Power," Steam Locomotive Research Institute, NY, 1947.
25. "The Steam Turbine: Coal's New Hope," page 15.
26. For a brief discussion of this concept locomotive see *N&W: Giant of Steam*, Major Lewis Ingles Jeffries, 1980, page 278 and the Pennsylvania Railroad's April 27, 1944, "Proposed Design of a 4-8-4-8 Freight Locomotive," which is available from the Norfolk & Western Historical Society as document HOL-00872.07.01. The "triplex" was also briefly featured in *Popular Mechanics*, July 1, 1945, page 17, and discussed in *Train Talks* (PRR Publication), April 1945, a copy of which is included in *Rails Remembered: Volume 4—The Tale of the Turbine*, Louis M. Newton, self-published, 2002, pages 714-716 (available from the Norfolk and Western Historical Society).
27. "Proposed Design of a 4-8-4-8 Freight Locomotive," page 1.
28. *Rails Remembered: Volume 4—The Tale of the Turbine*, pages 714-716.
29. For a discussion of this locomotive, see *C&O Power*, Alvin Staufer, 1965, pages 298-305; "This Was the Train That Was (But Never Was)," Geoffrey H. George, *Trains*, July 1968, pages 38-47; and other sources listed in the "Further Reading" section for this locomotive.
30. *The Chesapeake and Ohio Railway: A Concise History and Fact Book*, Thomas W. Dixon, Jr. (Chesapeake and Ohio Historical Society, Clifton Forge, Va., 2012), page 146.
31. M-1 length is shown differently from different sources. The 145-foot length is provided by Gene Huddleston in his, "The Genesis, Design, and Performance of C&O's Steam Turbo-Electric M-1—Part 2," *The Chesapeake and Ohio Historical Magazine*, C&O Historical Society, October 1997, page 3.
32. Ibid., page 7.
33. Huddleston reports that in a comparison run with C&O's 2-6-6-6 Allegheny steam locomotive, the M-1 consumed 21,907 gallons of water in one hour and 52 minutes. See "The Genesis, Design, and Performance of C&O's Steam Turbo-Electric M-1—Part 2," page 9.
34. Ibid., page 6.
35. "This Was the Train That Was (But Never Was)," page 47.
36. Ibid., pages 38-47.
37. For a comprehensive discussion of the Norfolk & Western TE-1 (Jawn Henry), see *Rails Remembered: Volume 4—The Tale of the Turbine*, Louis M. Newton, self-published, 2002. Also see *N&W: Giant of Steam*, pages 282-285, "Mallets to Jawn Henry," C.E. Pond, *Trains*, October 1984, and Baldwin Locomotive Works Specification No. 48-D-18 for "Baldwin Locomotive Works, Westinghouse Electric Corporation, Babcock & Wilcox Company 4,500 Horsepower Coal-Fired Steam Turbine Electric Drive Locomotive with Tender," available from the Norfolk & Western Historical Society as their document number HOL-00872.07.02.
38. John Henry is an African-American folk hero. According to his legend, he was a "steel drivin' man" who worked on the railroad blasting tunnels by manually hammering steel drills into rock to make holes for explosives. He was said to have beaten a steam drill in a race, though he died in the effort.
39. "Four Turbo-Locomotives That Were Built by Baldwin-Westinghouse and What Went Wrong," page 18.
40. *Rails Remembered: Volume 4—The Tale of the Turbine*, page 804.
41. "N&W's Secret Weapons," Robert A. Le Massena, *Trains*, November 1991, pages 64-69. The Y6c was a variant of the Y6b that Le Massena says received a "booster valve," which introduced higher temperature superheated steam into the locomotive's larger compound cylinders, and other improvements.
42. The combustion air would be heated by passing through tubes that crossed through the exhaust flow four times. Counterflow refers to the fact that the first tubes the exhaust flow would encounter would contain the warmest air.
43. The gas heater is mentioned in a N&W report reproduced in *Rails Remembered: Volume 4—The Tale of the Turbine*, page 729. The boiler diagram on page 722 shows the location of the gas heater within the exit portion of the boiler. These energy systems are also mentioned and discussed in Baldwin-Lima-Hamilton's Steam Turbine Electric Freight Locomotive with Dynamic Braking Operator's Manual for Norfolk & Western Railroad No. 2300, September 1954.
44. Baldwin Locomotive Works Specification No. 48-D-18, page 12.
45. *Rails Remembered Volume 4—The Tale of a Turbine*, page 774.
46. Ibid.
47. Ibid., page 775.
48. Ibid.
49. Ibid., page 770.
50. Ibid., page 767. Turbine inlet is given as 1,482 BTUs/pound of steam, extracted heat given as 251.5 BTUs/pound. 251.5 divided by 1,482 = 0.169 or 16.9%.
51. Ibid., page 770.
52. "Four Turbo-Locomotives That Were Built by Baldwin-Westinghouse and What Went Wrong," page 21.
53. *Rails Remembered: Volume 4—The Tale of the Turbine*, page 767. Calculation shows turbine shaft horsepower divided into 4,500 for traction and 170 horsepower for auxiliary purposes.
54. Ibid., 823.
55. Ibid., page 804.
56. "Mallets to Jawn Henry," page 44.
57. Ibid., pages 44-45.
58. *Rails Remembered: Volume 4—The Tale of the Turbine*, page 908.
59. Ibid., page 909.
60. Letters from N&W Superintendent of Motive Power "KVC" to Mr. H.C. Wyatt, N&W Vice President and General Manager, January 20 and February 17, 1955; and "Steam Turbine Electric Locomotive, Condensing Type with Evaporative Cooler, 7000 hp to Generators for Traction (Approximately 6,000 at the Rails)" Baldwin-Lima-Hamilton Corp. report, Philadelphia, Pa., May 25, 1955 (both available through the Norfolk & Western Historical Society).
61. Letters from N&W Superintendent of Motive Power.
62. "Steam Turbine Electric Locomotive, Condensing Type with Evaporative Cooler, 7000 hp to Generators for Traction."
63. As a point of comparison, consider that a reciprocating steam locomotive would consume (and lose to the atmosphere) 30,000 gallons of water for every 12 tons of coal it burned (assuming 75% boiler efficiency) and a UP Big Boy steam locomotive could consume 100,000 gallons of water per hour ("Horsepower Without Cylinders," David P. Morgan, *Trains*, March 1956, page 20.)
64. See helpful video at "Gas Turbine for Power Generation: Introduction," www.Wartsila.com. Also, see "Introduction to Gas Turbines for Non-Engineers," Lee S. Langston and George Opdyke, Jr., *Global Gas Turbine News*, Volume 37: 1997, No. 2.
65. For an excellent visual explanation of the turboshaft

gas turbine engine, see "How a Gas Turbine Works" from the Edison Tech Center.

66. "Gas Turbine Power," W. Giger, *Railway Mechanical Engineer*, October 1948, page 92 (574). This is an abstract of a paper presented to Power Division of the American Society of Mechanical Engineers, Portland, Ore., September 7-9, 1948 (*Train Shed Cyclopedia No. 80*).

67. *Turbines Westward*, page 22, where author Thomas. R Lee states that the 4,500 horsepower turbine engines consumed 600 gallons of Bunker C fuel per hour. This equates to 13% efficiency. See calculation in section about these UP Bunker oil-burning GTELs.

68. New York Central assumed 22% and Norfolk & Western assumed 23% as the overall optimal or design efficiency of diesel-electric locomotives in the late 1940s when comparing these locomotives to conventional reciprocating steam locomotives. See *A Practical Evaluation of Railroad Motive Power*, P.W. Kiefer, Steam Locomotive Research Institute, N.Y., 1947, page 60; and *N&W: Giant of Steam*, Major Lewis Ingles Jeffries, 1980, page 62.

69. *Turbines Westward*, page 22.

70. "Gas Turbine Power," page 93 (575).

71. *Turbines Westward*, page 13.

72. "What Type Motive Power," H.E. Dralle, *Railway Age*, January 1, 1949. (Dralle was manager of Transportation Application Engineering for the Westinghouse Electric Corporation. In this article his discussion of gas turbine motive power forshadows the Westinghouse Blue Goose locomotive, which was to debut in 1950.)

73. "Breaking the Power Plant Efficiency Record," GE Power, www.gepower.com.

74. *Turbines Westward*, page 23.

75. For a thorough discussion of the Union Pacific GE GTEL, see *Turbines Westward*. Additionally, David I. Smith's "The Gas Turbine Electric Locomotive Story" (1986) is an authoritative account but not publicly available. Smith was involved with the development of the gas turbine. In 1947, he became a test engineer and then in 1948 a member of GE's Locomotive Engineering Division in Erie, Pa. He was extensively involved in shop and road testing the GTELs for GE and UP. The author thanks Tom Leary for sharing a copy of this very interesting and at times amusing report. Also see "The Alco-GE Gas Turbine-Electric Locomotive," P.T. Egbert and G.W. Wilson, *Railway Mechanical Engineer*, July 1949 (available in *Train Shed Cyclopedia, No. 80*) and "Oil Burning Gas Turbine Locomotives," G.M. Davies (Locomotive Editor) *1966 Car and Locomotive Cyclopedia* (Simmons Boardman Publishing, New York, NY 1966), page 1061.

76. "The Gas Turbine Electric Locomotive Story," page 4.

77. Ibid.

78. David I. Smith ("The Gas Turbine Story") says 65%, and Thomas Lee (*Turbines Westward*) says 80%, page 22.

79. *Turbines Westward*, page 22.

80. Ibid., page 13.

81. Ibid.

82. *Turbines Westward*, page 12.

83. *Turbines Westward*, page 21.

84. Ibid., page 25.

85. "Operation of 8500-Hp Gas Turbines in Locomotive Service," H. Rees (Union Pacific Railroad), presented at Gas Turbine Power Conference, American Society of Mechanical Engineers, Washington, D.C., March 5-9, 1961, ASME paper 61-GTP-8, page 3.

86. "Oil Burning Gas Turbine Locomotives," G.M. Davies (Locomotive Editor) *1966 Car and Locomotive Cyclopedia* (Simmons Boardman Publishing, New York, NY 1966), page 1061.

87. "The Gas Turbine Electric Locomotive Story," page 17; and *Turbines Westward*, page 25.

88. David P. Morgan reported that the tenders were insulated with 4 inches of rock wool and were not heated. Instead, the Bunker C fuel was loaded warm. ("Horsepower Without Cylinders," page 21). Elsewhere, it was that the Bunker C fuel was pumped into the tenders at 180°F ("Oil Burning Gas Turbine Locomotive").

89. *Turbines Westward*, page 26.

90. "The Gas Turbine Electric Locomotive Story," page 15.

91. By one account, UP primarily burned No. 5 fuel oil. See "Using Bunker C as Locomotive Fuel," UtahRails. net, utahrails.net/up/bunker-c.php.

92. "The Propane Gas Turbine Research Project" edited by Thomas Lee, Union Pacific Historical Society's *The Streamliner, Summer 1994*.

93. *Turbines Westward*, pages 42-43.

94. Ibid., page 22.

95. "The Alco-GE Gas Turbine-Electric Locomotive," page 366.

96. *Turbines Westward*, pages 42-43.

97. Ibid.

98. Ibid and "The Alco-GE Gas Turbine-Electric Locomotive," page 368.

99. *Big Blow: Union Pacific's Super Turbines*, the Rev. Harold Keekley (George R. Cockle and Associates, Omaha Neb., 1975), page 11.

100. *Turbines Westward*, pages 43-44.

101. "Evaluation of the Gas Turbine Electric Locomotive," Gibbs & Hill Consulting Engineers, March 27, 1953.

102. Ibid., pages 4-5, 27-44.

103. Ibid., pages 3-4, 22-24.

104. Ibid., pages 5, 12-13, 22-24.

105. Ibid., pages 4, 11-20.

106. Ibid., pages 4, 14.

107. For discussions of the Westinghouse-Baldwin Blue Goose GTEL, see "The Thrifty Glutton," David P. Morgan, *Trains and Travel*, January 1953; *Turbines Westward*, pages 48-49 (referenced previously); "4000-hp Gas Turbines Passenger Locomotives," W.A. Brecht, Charles Kerr, Jr.; T.J. Putz, *Railway Mechanical and Electrical Engineer*, January 1950 (available in *Train Shed Cyclopedia, No.80*); "Turbine Locomotives," www.classicstreamliners.com/lo-turbines.html; and "Four Turbo-Locomotives That Were Built by Baldwin-Westinghouse and What Went Wrong," page 22.

108. "The Gas Turbine as Railroad Motive Power," J. K. Hodnette (Vice President, Westinghouse Corporation) November 12, 1952, luncheon address, Chicago, Ill., following inspection of the Blue Goose by railroad officials.

109. "Progress Report—Baldwin-Westinghouse Gas-Turbine Electric Locomotive," T.J. Putz (Manager, Locomotive and Gas Turbine Engineering Division, Westinghouse Corp.), *Power Engineering*, November 1951 and "Westinghouse Gas-Turbine Locomotive," (no author listed), *Diesel Railway Traction*, June, 1954, pages 142-145.

110. "The Gas Turbine as Railroad Motive Power."

111. "4,000-Hp Gas Turbines Passenger Locomotives," page 3.

112. Ibid., page 1.

113. "The Thrifty Glutton," page 25.

114. *Turbines Westward*, page 49. Note: The locomotive's weight is given at 460,000 pounds in "Thrifty Glutton."

115. "4,000-Hp Gas Turbines Passenger Locomotives," page 4.

116. Ibid., page 5.

117. Ibid.

118. Ibid., page 3.

119. "Four Turbo-Locomotives That Were Built by Baldwin-Westinghouse and What Went Wrong," page 22.

120. "4,000-Hp Gas Turbines Passenger Locomotives," page 2.

121. "Westinghouse Gas-Turbine Locomotive," page 144.

122. "Four Turbo-Locomotives That Were Built by Baldwin-Westinghouse and What Went Wrong," page 22. However, technically speaking, it could be argued that this was not a combined cycle because the steam produced in the heat recovery unit was not used to generate additional electricity for traction or other purposes onboard the locomotives.

123. "Thrifty Glutton," page 28.

124. Ibid.

125. "Operating Record of the Westinghouse-Baldwin Gas Turbine Locomotive," Charles Kerr, Jr., T.J. Putz, and T.L. Weybrew (all of the Westinghouse Corporation), presented at the annual meeting of the American Society of Mechanical Engineers, November 30-December 5, 1952.

126. "Progress Report—Baldwin-Westinghouse Gas-Turbine Electric Locomotive," page 113-114.

127. "A 4,000 hp Gas Turbine Locomotive for Passenger Service," W.A. Brecht, Charles Kerr, Jr.; T.J. Putz, presented at the annual meeting of the American Society of Mechanical Engineers, November 27-December 2, 1949, page 5.

128. Ibid.

129. For a discussion of the UP's coal-burning gas turbine locomotive, see Thomas Lee's *Turbines Westward*, pages 32-34 and "Coal Burning Gas Turbine Locomotive," G.M. Davies (Locomotive Editor), *1966 Car and Locomotive Cyclopedia* (Simmons Boardman Publications, New York, NY, 1966), pages 1058-1059. For a more comprehensive account, see Lee's "Coal-Burning Gas Turbine-Electric Locomotive" in the Union Pacific Historical Society's *The Streamliner, Volume 16, No. 4* (Fall 2002).

130. Turbines Westward, page 32.

131. Ibid., pages 32-34.

132. Ibid., page 33.

133. Ibid., page 34.

134. "Coal-Burning Gas Turbine-Electric Locomotive," page 22.

135. See "Gas Turbine Power" (cited previously) and "Gas Turbine Locomotive," John L. Yellott and Charles F. Kotteamp, from a paper presented to Railway Fuel and Traveling Engineers' Association, Chicago, September 6, 1946 (*Train Shed Cyclopedia No. 66*), pages 615-620). The former, "Gas Turbine Power," dated 1948, describes the proposed turbine as 4,120 horsepower while the latter, "Gas Turbine Locomotive," dated 1946, describes it as 3,750 horsepower. No reason is given for the discrepancy. Incidentally, John Yellott was Director of Research for Bituminous Coal Research Inc. Also: "Future Fuels and Engines for Railroad Locomotives," S.G. Liddle et. al., Jet Propulsion Laboratory, California Institute of Technology (prepared for the U.S. Department of Energy), November 1, 1981; "Design of Advanced Coal-Fired Gas Turbine Locomotives," Sidney G. Liddle, California Engineering Research Institute, ASME 85-IGT-48, 1985; and Coal-Fired Gas Turbine for Locomotive Propulsion," Leon Green, Jr., Energy Conversion Alternatives, Ldt., ASME 87-GT-273, 1987.

136. "Turbines—King Coal's Battle against the Diesel," Eric Hirsimaki, *Classic Trains*, Fall 2004.

137. "Postwar Parade: 2," A.C. Kalmbach, *Trains*, November 1945, page 33.

138. "Mallets to Jawn Henry," page 43.

139. "More Power on Wheels: Diesel, Steam or Turbine, A Huskier Iron Horse Emerges from a Quiet Revolution of Railroading," Devon Francis, *Popular Science*, October 1946, pages 66-72.

140. "Fuel Oil for Diesel Locomotives," a Report by Electro-Motive Division and Research Laboratories Division of General Motors Corporation, September 25, 1948.

141. "Turbines—King Coal's Battle Against the Diesel," page 26.

142. "Gas Turbine Power."

143. "Gas Turbine Locomotive," page 620.

144. "Turbines—King Coal's Battle against the Diesel," page 35.

145. "Bureau of Mines Coal-Fired Gas Turbine Research Project: Redesign and Assembly of Turbine," J.P. McGee, J. Smith, R.W. Cargill, and D.C. Strimbeck, 1961 manuscript. Note that the Department of Mines was part of the U.S. Department of Interior. It was closed in 1995 with some of its functions transferred to the U.S. Department of Energy.

146. Stellite, a trademarked name of the Kennametal

Stellite Company, is a cobalt-chromium alloy designed to resist wear.

147. The previously referenced Cal Tech report "Future Fuels and Engines for Railroad Locomotives" is a case in point. Immediately after observing that American railroads are dependent on Diesel No. 2 fuel, the report states that, "This fuel oil has changed from a relatively cheap and readily available commodity to one having an increasingly limited supply and higher cost. There has been, therefore, a growing interest in improving fuel economy of locomotives and in finding alternative fuels for use in these same engines." The report reaches the conclusion that "A coal-fired locomotive using any one of a number of engines appears to be the best alternative to the diesel-electric locomotive with regard to life-cycle cost, fuel availability, and development risk."

148. For example, see "Alco-GE Gas Turbine-Electric Completes Preliminary Tests," *Railway Age*, June 18, 1949, page 85, which states that "Alco-GE spokesmen previously had expressed hopes that special research efforts, joined with experience gained from operation of the first (GTEL) locomotive design, may lead to the development of successful means of burning coal in a gas turbine-electric locomotive."

149. "Economic Assessment of Coal Burning Locomotives," General Electric Company, U.S. Department of Energy report (contract number DE-AC21-85MC22181), 1986.

150. A fluidized bed coal boiler combines coal fuel, coal ash, and limestone in a combustion bed, which is fluidized by combustion air jets that inject air from below the bed, thus suspending and continuously mixing it. The addition of limestone reduces acid-rain-producing sulfur dioxide emissions. Lower combustion temperatures also reduce nitrogen oxide emissions, which also contribute to acid rain, smog, and respiratory illness.

151. A two-spooling gas turbine has low and high pressure compression fans in the front section of the engine and high and low pressure turbines in the back of the engine. Through the use of concentric shafts (one inside the other) the high-pressure fans and turbines are connected to one another and turn at the same speed, while the low-pressure fans and blades, which are also connected to one another, turn at another (slower) speed. This compound arrangement adds to the output and efficiency of the turbine, including at part-load.

152. For a comprehensive discussion of the NYC jet engine-powered Budd railcar, see "The Flight of the M-497: How the New York Central Railroad Set the U.S. Speed Record for a Passenger Train in July 1966," Hank Morris and Don Wetzel, 2007 (now published as a book by Lulu Press); "Whoosh! What the Pride of the Central Was ... and Wasn't," Chuck Crouse, *Trains*, February, 1989; "The Jet Train Roars Back: Don Wetzel Talks about His Record Breaking Ride, Jet-Powered Snowblowers and LEGOmaniacs," GE Reports, Thomas Keller, February 14, 2014; NYC Jet Car M-497 (YouTube video); and "New York Central M-497 Jet Train," Donald C. and Ruth Wetzel, PowerPoint.

153. "The Flight of the M-497," page 11 with additional input from Don Wetzel.

154. Ibid, pages 13-15.

155. Email exchange with Don Wetzel, October 10, 2018.

156. Email exchanges with Don Wetzel, October 2018.

157. "GT-2 Test Car Undergoing Daily Runs on Long Island Tracks for High Speed Commuter Service," NY Metropolitan Transportation Authority press release, July 29, 1970; "LIRR GT 1/2 Gas Turbine Cars," from the, "gas turbine cars" section of www.trainsarefun.com website; and "L.I.R.R Awaiting Gas-Turbine Cars," Edward C. Burks, *New York Times*, January 26, 1975. For technical assessment of GT/E M1 cars, see "Dual-Powered Gas Turbine/Electric Commuter Rail Cars: Test, Evaluations, and Economics," Donald Raskin, Charles Stark, and L.T. Klauder & Associates (prepared for the New York Metropolitan Transportation Authority under the sponsorship of the

U.S. Urban Mass Transportation Authority, USDOT), September 1980. The latter report is available by interlibrary loan. The author's research librarian obtained a copy from the Northwestern University Library.

158. "GT-2 Test Car Undergoing Daily Runs on Long Island Tracks for High Speed Commuter Service," page 2.

159. "Here's an Invitation for a Turbine Ride," *Long Island Railroader*, September 22, 1966, page 2.

160. "Dual-Powered Gas Turbine/Electric Commuter Rail Cars: Test, Evaluations, and Economics," page 4.

161. "Car in L.I.R.R. Test Develops Gas Pains," *New York Times*, April 12, 1970.

162. "LIRR GT 1/2 Gas Turbine Cars," scroll to bottom of page.

163. "Dual-Powered Gas Turbine/Electric Commuter Rail Cars: Test, Evaluations, and Economics," pages 8, 19, and 26.

164. Ibid., page 39.

165. Ibid., page 45.

166. For a thorough discussions of Amtrak TurboTrains, see *TurboTrain: A Journey*, Jason Shron, Rapido Trains Inc., 2007; "The TurboTrain Story," Marc J. Frattasio, *NHRHTA Shoreliner, Volume 29, Issue 2* and 3 (2002); "TURBOTRAIN: Is the Hardware Equal to the Hard Sell?," Harold Edmonson, *Trains*, April 1969; "United Aircraft's Turbo Train: The Transfer of Aerospace Technology to Rail Transportation," Michael P. Chaney (Railroad History, Railroad & Locomotive Historical Society, Spring 1986); "The Turbotrain Revisited," William D. Middleton, *Trains*, March 1970, page 32; "The Fading Days of the Turbo," El Simon Jr., *Passenger Train Journal*, July 1996; the "TurboTrain" page of the online Sikorsky Archives; "TurboTrain: Can It Put Profit in Passengers?" F. N. Houser, *Railway Age*, June 19, 1967; Wikipedia entry UAC TurboTrain and the Wikipedia entry for Turboliner; history.amtrak.com; "CN Turbotrain—3:59—The Lost Film," YouTube video; and *The World's Fastest Trains—from the Age of Steam to the TVG*, Geoffrey Freeman Allen (Ian Allan Ltd/Patrick Stephens Limited, 1978 and 1992), pages 140-143.

167. "TURBOTRAIN: Is the Hardware Equal to the Hard Sell?," pages 20-21.

168. "A New Fast Turbine Train," *Railway Age*, December 6, 1965, pages 11-12.

169. *World' Fastest Trains*, page 140.

170. "TURBOTRAIN: Is the Hardware Equal to the Hard Sell?," page 22.

171. "TURBOTRAIN: Is the Hardware Equal to the Hard Sell?," page 20; and "Second Chance for Turbo," William D. Middleton, *Trains*, June 1971, page 30.

172. Regarding the reference to "free turbine" and "aerodynamic torque converter," see "TurboTrain: Can It Put Profit in Passengers?" and Wikipedia entry "UAC TurboTrain." A free turbine design has two disconnected shafts, each with its own rows of rotating turbines. The turbines mounted on the first shaft power the turbine engine's compressor. The turbines on the second shaft provide output horsepower.

173. "The Turbotrain Revisited," page 34. Incidentally, Middleton describes the TurboTrain's transmission as "a system of gear boxes and cardan shafts."

174. *TurboTrain: A Journey*, page 124.

175. Unsprung weight is weight that is not supported by the trucks' springs, e.g. wheels, axles, and a portion of the trucks themselves and electric traction motors. Unsprung weight is a detriment to the handling of the truck. It increases the locomotive's impact on the track, especially in curves, on poorly aligned track, at higher speeds, and when trucks "hunt" between the rails.

176. "TurboTrain: Can It Put Profit in Passengers?"

177. *TurboTrain: A Journey*, page 133.

178. "TurboTrain" page of the online Sikorsky Archives.

179. "TurboTrain Revisited," page 32.

180. Ibid., page 35. Also, "The TurboTrain Story," Marc J. Frattasio, *NHRHTA Shoreliner, Volume 29, Issue 2* (2002).

181. "The TurboTrain Story," page 15.

182. "The Man Behind the Train" sidebar in "Turbotrain Revisited," page 34

183. "Who Shot the Passenger Train," David P. Morgan, *Trains*, April 1959, pages 36-39.

184. *TurboTrain: A Journey*, pages 13-16.

185. "TurboTrain: Can It Put Profit in Passengers?"

186. "High Speed Rail Transportation in North America, joint webpage of the Institute of Electrical and Electronics Engineers (IEEE) and the American Society of Mechanical Engineers (ASME) celebrating the June 14, 2007, installation of a plaque along Amtrak's Northeast Corridor at Princeton Junction, N.J.

187. *TurboTrain: A Journey*, page 38-42.

188. "TurboTrain" page of the online Sikorsky Archives.

189. TurboTrains for the New York Central System, United Aircraft Corporate Systems Center, September 27, 1967.

190. Ibid.

191. *World's Fastest Trains*, page 143.

192. "Second Chance for Turbo," page 30.

193. For a thorough discussion of Amtrak Turboliners, see *Trail of the Turbo: The Amtrak Turboliner Story*, Dale A. Johnson (self-published, 2016, available through Amazon); "Americanizing the Turboliner," William D. Middleton, *Railway Age*, April 14, 1975; "The American Turboliner," J. R. Pier, presented at the Gas Turbine Conference and Products Show, March 2-6, 1975, Houston, Tex., ASME 75-GT-108; "The American Turboliner: A Progress Report," Jerome R. Pier, presented at the Gas Turbine and Aeroengine Congress and Exposition, June 4-8, 1989, Toronto, Canada, ASME report 89-GT-110; "The Fading Days of the Turbo," El Simon Jr., *Passenger Train Journal*, July 1996; and the Wikipedia entry Turboliner. Amtrak's history.amtrak.com also contains some information and images.

194. "SNCF Class T 2000," Wikipedia entry.

195. "The American Turboliner," page 4.

196. "The American Turboliner: A Progress Report," page 2. However, the engineer did have the option of operating one power car with more power output than the other. This could be desirable when accelerating. Then, the second power car would have more adhesion (and thus be able to handle more power without wheel slippage) as a result of operating over rail warmed by the first power car and passenger cars—as per conversation with retired Amtrak Turboliner maintenance supervisor/mechanical superintendent, December 27, 2018.

197. Conversation with retired Amtrak Turboliner maintenance supervisor/mechanical superintendent.

198. *Trail of the Turbo: The Amtrak Turboliner Story*, pages 16 and 34.

199. "The American Turboliner: A Progress Report," page 2.

200. "Americanizing the Turboliner," page 27 and *Trail of the Turbo: The Amtrak Turboliner Story*, page 16.

201. Ibid.

202. Ibid.

203. Conversation with retired Amtrak Turboliner maintenance supervisor/mechanical superintendent.

204. "The Turbotrain," ANF Industrie Group (undated company brochure).

205. Amtrak postcard depicting the RTG turboliner.

206. See amtrak.history.com and search "turboliners".

207. *Trail of the Turbo: The Amtrak Turboliner Story*, page 32.

208. Ibid., footnote 4, page 41.

209. "The American Turboliner: A Progress Report," page 2.

210. Information provided by Bruce B. Becker, Vice-President, Passenger Rail Association, and Amtrak Turboliner maintenance supervisor/mechanical superintendent. The 10 operational Turboliners were three RTG IIs and 7 RTLs.

211. "The American Turboliner: A Progress Report," page 3.

212. Ibid., page 4; and "Test Train for Fuel Conservation and Time Delay," January 29, 1980, Amtrak memo.

213. "The American Turboliner," page 6.

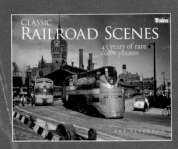

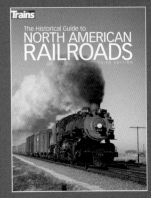

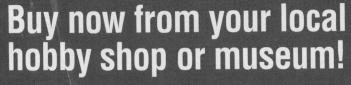

214. Conversation with retired Amtrak Turboliner supervisor/mechanical superintendent.

215. These fuel consumption numbers include diesel fuel consumed for head-end-power, or HEP, purposes.

216. Conversation with retired Amtrak Turboliner maintenance supervisor/mechanical superintendent.

217. *Trail of the Turbo: The Amtrak Turboliner Story*, page 42.

218. "Report on the RTL-2 Turboliner High-Speed Demonstration," Federal Railroad Administration, August 9, 1995.

219. Ibid., page 4; and conversation with retired Amtrak Turboliner maintenance supervisor/mechanical superintendent.

220. Ibid., page 8.

221. Ibid.

222. "Report on the Testing of an Upgraded Turbine Trainset," Edward J. Lombardi and Janice P. Li, Mechanical and Engineering Services, Philadelphia, Pa., Amtrak, March 10, 1995, page 7.

223. *Trail of the Turbo: The Amtrak Turboliner Story*, page 122.

224. Conversation with retired Amtrak Turboliner maintenance supervisor/mechanical superintendent.

225. "Comparative Economic Assessment of a Natural Gas Fueled Locomotive with On-Board CNG Storage to Diesel and LNG Variants," Frank Donnelly et. al. paper presented at IEEE/ASME Joint Railroad Conference, Baltimore, Md., April 6, 1995 (14 authors from these companies: Applied Power & Propulsion, AlliedSignal Corporation, Allison Engine Company/Rolls-Royce Aerospace Group, BC Rail, and EDO Energy Company); "Major Study Confirms 'Staggering' 37% Fuel Cost Savings for U.S. Class 1 Railroads Using Compressed Natural Gas Instead of Diesel," Applied Power & Propulsion press release, April 6, 1995; and "A Concept for a Natural Gas Fueled Locomotive that Uses a Gas Turbine," F.W. Donnelly, SAE Technical Paper Series #891699, presented at Future Transportation Technology Conference and Exposition, Vancouver, British Columbia, August 7-10, 1989.

226. Conversation with Peter Roosen, former President of Applied Power and Propulsion.

227. "Comparative Economic Assessment of a Natural Gas Fueled Locomotive with On-Board CNG Storage to Diesel and LNG Variants," page 19.

228. Conversation with Peter Roosen and Frank Donnelly.

229. Typically, a 60% to 80% natural gas blend. Up to 95% natural gas is now possible.

230. "Comparative Economic Assessment of a Natural Gas Fueled Locomotive with On-Board CNG Storage to Diesel and LNG Variants," page 9.

231. Ibid.

232. Ibid., page 12. These lightweight cylinders were the product of a research and development program undertaken by the Canadian government, further designed and manufactured by EDO Energy Corporation.

233. Ibid, page 3-4.

234. "Comparative Economic Assessment of a Natural Gas Fueled Locomotive with On-Board CNG Storage to Diesel and LNG Variants," page 12. The 7,788 BTU/hp-hr fuel flow rate for full power operation given in Table 5 equates to 2,544 BTU/7,788 = 0.326 or 32.6%, where 2,544 is the number of BTUs in one hp-hr of work.

235. Assumptions: SD60 BSFC = 0.34 pounds/hp-hr; Energy density of diesel fuel = 18,358 BTU/pound (lower heating value); And hp-hr – 2,544 BTU. Energy efficiency = work output / energy input. Work output = 2,544 BTU. Input energy = 0.34 x 18,358 = 6,242 BTU. Energy efficiency = 2,544 / 6,242 = 0.408 = 40.8%.

236. Ibid.

237. "A Concept for a Natural Gas Fueled Locomotive that Uses a Gas Turbine," pages 3-6.

238. "Comparative Economic Assessment of a Natural Gas Fueled Locomotive with On-Board CNG Storage to Diesel and LNG Variants," page 19.

239. Conversation with Peter Roosen.

240. "Major Study Confirms 'Staggering' 37% Fuel Cost Savings for U.S. Class 1 Railroads Using Compressed Natural Gas Instead of Diesel."

241. "Gas Turbine is on Track," Mark Wilson, *Sunday Province*, April 9, 1995, page A45.

242. See Wikipedia entry JetTrain.

243. See Wikipedia entry Gas Turbine-Electric Locomotives.

244. Bombardier press release and fact sheets, October 15, 2002.

245. Ibid.

246. Ibid. This test speed was reported in a number of other publications including *Trains*, January 2009, page 70. Also, Bombardier October 15, 2002, press release.

247. "Technology Comparison: High Speed Ground Transportation—Transrapid Superspeed Maglev and Bombardier JetTrain," American Magline Group, December 2002, page 12.

248. Ibid.

249. Wikipedia "JetTrain."

250. Ibid. and "Bombardier Unveils JetTrain Technology," Bombardier press release, October 15, 2002. (Archived on www.railway-technology.com).

251. Bombardier press release and facts sheets, October 15, 2002.

252. Ibid.

253. Head-end-power, or HEP, refers to the energy supply within the locomotive, which supplies passenger car lighting, heating, cooling, and ventilation.

254. Wikipedia entry "JetTrain."

255. http://turbotrain.net/en/jettrain.htm.

256. See Wikipedia entry "Development of the TGV" said to be based on information from TGVweb; also Wikipedia entry on "TGV 001" and Trainweb.org's "Early TGV History;" and "Tests Undertaken with Turbine Train TGV 001," J. Gouley, *Proceedings of the Institution of Mechanical Engineers, Volume 191, Issue 1*, June 1, 1977. Also, *The World's Fastest Trains*, page 155. In French: see articles "Le Turbotrain Experimental TGV 001" and "Les Essais du TGV 001" in the April and July 1972 issues, respectively, of *La Vie du Rail*.

257. TGV is the French acronym for "Train a Grande Vitesse" or, literally, "high speed train." The extensive TGV high-speed rail network is operated by SNCF, France's national rail operator.

258. Wikipedia entry on "TGV 001."

259. "Early TGV History" and www.trainweb.org; and "Tests Undertaken with Turbine Train TGV 001," which explain that various turbine engines were tried. The initial gas turbine engine produced 1,800 KW or 2,400 horsepower. Two of them provided the trainset with 4,800 horsepower. Eventually, the Turmo XII B turbine was used. It was rated at 2,400 KW (3,200 horsepower), yielding 6,400 horsepower for the trainset.

260. "Le Turbotrain Experimental TGV 001," *La Vie du Rail*, April, 1972.

261. *The World's Fastest Trains*, page 155.

262. Wikipedia entry on "TGV 001." Also see "Tests Undertaken with Turbine Train TGV 001" where 165 is given as the number of test runs at or above 300 kph.

263. *The World's Fastest Trains*, page 155.

264. For thorough discussions of Lyle Borst's X-12 atomic locomotive, see "An Atomic Locomotive—A Feasibility Study," G.K. Abel, L.B. Borst, et. al., Department of Physics, University of Utah, January 1, 1954; "Dr. Borst's X-12: The Atomic Locomotive," Thornton Waite, *Railroad History #175*, Autumn 1996; "To Peoria by Atom: Atomic Powered-Locomotive," Atomic Skies Blog, Mark J. Appleton, July 2, 2012; "The Atomic Locomotive," Lyle Borst and K. W. Petty, *Railway Progress*, July 1954; "An Atomic Locomotive Could Be Built," *Popular Science*, April 1954, page 137; and "The Atomic Locomotive," Lyle Borst and K.W. Petty, *Railway Progress*, July 1954.

265. The full text of President Dwight D. Eisenhower's "Atoms of Peace" speech and various background documents are available from the Eisenhower Presidential Library, eisenhower.archives.gov/research/online_documents/atoms_for_peace.html.

266. See "More Power on Wheels: Diesel, Steam or Turbine, A Huskier Iron Horse Emerges from a Quiet Revolution of Railroading," page 72. Alco research staff member R. Tom Sawyer is quoted saying at the 1946 American Society of Mechanical Engineers conference in Charleston, W.Va., that "There is no question in my mind that the atomic powered locomotive will be used on long, through runs eventually."

267. "An Atomic Locomotive—A Feasibility Study."

268. "Lyle Borst, 89, Nuclear Physicist Who Worked on A-Bomb Project, *New York Times* (Obituary), Anahad O'Connor, August 1, 2002.

269. "The Atomic Locomotive."

270. "An Atomic Locomotive Could Be Built," page 276.

271. "An Atomic Locomotive—A Feasibility Study," page 25.

272. Ibid., page 14.

273. While 7,000 horsepower is used in various other articles, in Borst's initial "An Atomic Locomotive—A Feasibility Study," he states that the X-12 would produce 7,200 horsepower for traction purposes, i.e. as delivered to the generator, page 11.

274. For example, see "The Atomic Locomotive," (referenced above) page 8.

275. Direct current electric traction motor continuous ratings are amperage levels that the motors can operate at continuously without thermal damage. Direct current traction motors also have short-term ratings, which reflect the higher levels of current and heat they can endure for shorter duration, e.g. 15 minutes, without damage. Higher amperage equates to greater horsepower output.

276. "An Atomic Locomotive Could Be Built," page 138.

277. "An Atomic Locomotive—A Feasibility Study," page 51.

278. "The Atomic Locomotive," page 9.

279. "Atomic Locomotive Quiz," Edward Kehoe, *Trains*, July 1955, page 21-23.

280. Florida East Coast Railway has employed a similar strategy by running a small fleet of dual-fuel diesel and natural gas locomotives on its Jacksonville to Miami, Fla., route, with no locomotive interchange with other railroads.

281. "Fracking: NRDC Policy Basics," Natural Resources Defense Council, February 2013.

282. Carbon dioxide and methane are both greenhouse gases that absorb heat and contribute to warming of the earth's atmosphere. But, comparing them on an equal mass basis, methane has 28 to 36 times the global warming potential of carbon dioxide over a 100-year time period, and, significantly, 84 to 87 times the global warming potential of CO_2 over the crucial 20-year time frame. The extreme global warming potential of methane would be of no consequence if all the natural gas produced was burned, and thus turned into carbon dioxide and water, but it is not. Some methane is released into the atmosphere when natural gas is produced, processed, and distributed. The Environmental Protection Agency's current estimates of methane leakage are in the 1% to 1.5% range. This sounds modest, but methane's global warming impact is significant for the reasons given above. Other studies have found that the EPA has underestimated methane leakage. A study conducted by the Environmental Defense Fund found that methane leakage rates were probably in the 1.5% to 2.5% range. Robert Howarth at Cornell University and colleagues have concluded that methane leakage associated with natural gas production is probably high enough to make the GHG footprint of natural gas greater than both diesel fuel and coal.